FOREST TRAILS AND HIGHWAYS OF THE MOUNT HOOD REGION

THE CLASSIC 1920 GUIDE TO CAMPING AND HIKING THE MT. HOOD NATIONAL FOREST AND WILDERNESS IN OREGON

BY THE **U.S. FOREST SERVICE**

ORIGINALLY PUBLISHED IN 1920

LEGACY EDITION

HISTORIC AMERICAN OUTDOORS DESTINATIONS SERIES
BOOK 1

FEATURING REMASTERED CLASSIC WORKS ILLUSTRATING

THE LEGENDARY DESTINATIONS OF THE UNMATCHED

AMERICAN OUTDOORS, FORESTS, PARKS, AND WILDERNESSES

Doublebit Press
Eugene, OR

INTRODUCTION

About the Historic American Outdoors Destinations Series Legacy Edition

The old experts of the woods and mountains taught timeless principles and skills for decades. Through their books, the old experts offered rich descriptions of the outdoor world and encouraged learning through personal experiences in nature. Over the last 125 years, camping, outdoors recreation, and woods activities have substantially changed. Many things have gotten simpler as gear has improved, and life outside or on the trail now brings with it many of the same comforts enjoyed in town. In addition, some activities of the olden days are now no longer in vogue, or are even outright considered inappropriate or illegal, such as high-impact camping practices like chopping down live trees. However, despite many of the positive changes in outdoors methods that have occurred over the years, *there are many other skills and much knowledge that have been forgotten* from the golden era of American outdoors recreation.

By publishing the Historic American Outdoors Destinations Series, it is our goal at Doublebit Press to do what we can to preserve and share the works from forgotten teachers that form the cornerstone of the history of the American outdoors. Through remastered reprint editions of timeless classics of outdoor recreation, perhaps we can regain some of this lost knowledge for future generations.

Because there were fewer options for finding outdoors gear in the early 1900's, experts in *"woodcraft"* skills (not to be confused with today's use of the word to mean woodworking or making things of wood) had to have a deep knowledge of the basic building blocks of outdoor living. This involved not only surviving in the outdoors, but to also have a comfortable and enjoyable time. As Nessmuk puts it in his book *Woodcraft,* "We do not go to the woods to rough it; we go to smooth it — we get it rough enough in town. But let us live the simple, natural life in the woods, and leave all frills behind." Nessmuk did not advocate for folks to go outside and have a terrible time. That would be contrary to the whole point of getting outside. Instead, he advocated for a "simpler" life by leaving some of the creature comforts of the city behind, but also entering the outdoors in a smart and practiced way that made the experience a much more satisfying vacation from home. The goal is to be comfortable so you can focus on having a good time outside and take in everything exposure to nature can offer. However, to be comfortable, one has to know the ins and outs of camping and outdoors life. Despite all the advances in campcraft and outdoors recreation, the old masters of the woods would all likely argue that this will only come from practicing the basics.

Because there was no market yet for specialty outdoors recreational gear (and thus, few outfitters), most outdoors gear came from military surplus piles or was custom made. As such, the old masters of woodcraft often made their own gear suited to their tastes. Through much experience in the woods and field, the great outdoors experts had to know why things worked the way they did by understanding the great web of cause and effect in nature. They had to learn from experience why certain gear worked better in different conditions or know how to solve problems off-the-cuff when things got hairy. They used the basic blocks of camping and outdoors knowledge to fine-tune their gear. They gained experience whenever they could and tried things different ways so they could gain mastery over the fundamentals and see challenges from many angles.

Today, much of the outdoor experience has been greatly simplified by neatly arranged campsites at public campgrounds and gear that has been meticulously improved and tested in both the lab and the field. Many modern conveniences are only a brief trek away, with many parks, campgrounds, and even forests having easy-access roads, convenience stores, and even cell phone signal. In some ways, it is much easier to camp and go outdoors today, and that is a good thing! We should not be miserable when we go outside — lovers of the outdoors know the essential restorative capability that the woods can have on the body, mind, and soul. Although things have gotten easier on us in the 21ˢᵗ Century when it comes to the outdoors, it certainly does not mean that we should forget the foundations of outdoors lore, though. All modern camping skills, outdoors equipment, and cool gizmos that make our lives easier are all founded on principles of the outdoors that the old masters knew well and taught to those who would listen.

Every woods master had their own curriculum or thought some things were more important than others. This includes the present author — certain things appear in this book that other masters leave out of theirs. The old masters also taught common things in slightly different ways or did things differently than others. That's what makes each of the experts different and worth reading. There's no universal way of doing something, especially now. Learning to go about something differently helps with mastery or learn a new skill altogether. Again, to use the metaphor from the above paragraphs, outdoors skills mastery consists of learning the basic building blocks of outdoors living, woods and nature lore, and the art of packing properly for trips. Each master goes about describing these building blocks differently or shows a different aspect of them.

Therefore, we have decided to publish this Legacy Edition in our Historic American Outdoors Destinations Series. This book is an important contribution to the early American recreational outdoors literature and has important historical and collector value toward preserving the American outdoors tradition. The knowledge it holds is an invaluable reference for practicing skills and hand craft methods. Its chapters thoroughly discuss some of the essential building blocks of knowledge that are fundamental but may have been forgotten as equipment gets fancier and technology gets smarter. In short, this book was chosen for Legacy Edition printing because much of the basic skills and knowledge it contains has been forgotten or put to the wayside in trade for more modern conveniences and methods.

Although the editors at Doublebit Press are thrilled to have comfortable experiences in the woods and love our high-tech and light-weight equipment, we are also realizing that the basic skills taught by the old masters are more essential than ever as our culture becomes more and more hooked on digital stuff. We don't want to risk forgetting the important steps, skills, or building blocks involved with thriving in the outdoors. The Legacy Edition series represents the essential contributions to the American outdoors tradition by the great experts of outdoors life and traditional hand crafting.

With technology playing a major role in everyday life, sometimes we need to take a step back in time to find those basic building blocks used for gaining mastery - the things that we have luckily not completely lost and has been recorded in books over the last two centuries. These skills aren't forgotten, they've just been shelved. *It's time to unshelve them once again and reclaim the lost knowledge of self-sufficiency.*

Based on this commitment to preserving our outdoors and handcraft heritage, we have taken great pride in publishing this book as a complete original work. We hope it is worthy of both study and collection by outdoors folk in the modern era of outdoors and traditional skills life.

Unlike many other photocopy reproductions of classic books that are common on the market, this Legacy Edition does not simply place poor photography of old texts on our pages and use error-prone optical scanning or computer-generated text. We want our work to speak for itself, and reflect the quality demanded by our customers who spend their hard-earned money. With this in mind, each Legacy Edition book that has been chosen for publication is carefully remastered from original print books, *with the Doublebit Legacy Edition printed and laid out in the exact way that it was presented at its original publication.* We provide a beautiful, memorable experience that is as true to the original text as best as possible, but with the aid of modern technology to make as beautiful a reading experience as possible for books that are typically over a century old.

Because of its age and because it is presented in its original form, the book may contain misspellings, inking errors, and other print blemishes that were common for the age. However, these are exactly the things that we feel give the book its character, which we preserved in this Legacy Edition. During digitization, we ensured that each illustration in the text was clean and sharp with the least amount of loss from being copied and digitized as possible. Full-page plate illustrations are presented as they were found, often including the extra blank page that was often behind a plate. For the covers, we use the original cover design to give the book its original feel. We are sure you'll appreciate the fine touches and attention to detail that your Legacy Edition has to offer.

For outdoors enthusiasts who demand the best from their equipment, this Doublebit Press Legacy Edition reprint was made with you in mind. Both important and minor details have equally both been accounted for by our publishing staff, down to the cover, font, layout, and images. It is the goal of Doublebit Legacy Edition series to preserve outdoors heritage, but also be cherished as collectible pieces, worthy of collection in any outdoorsperson's library and that can be passed to future generations.

Every book selected to be in this series offers unique views and instruction on important skills, advice, tips, tidbits, anecdotes, stories, and experiences that will enrich the repertoire of any person who enjoys escaping the city and finding their way to the trails of the wilds. To learn the most basic building blocks of outdoors life leads to mastery of all its aspects.

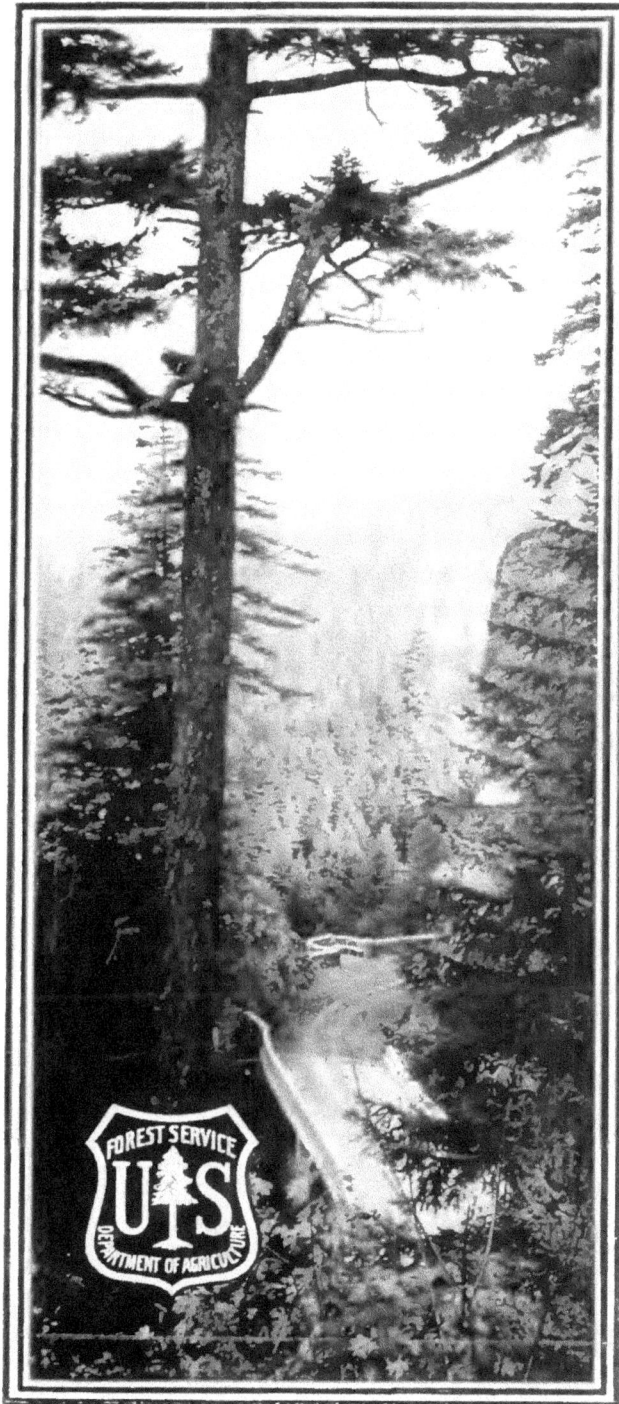

FOREST TRAILS AND HIGHWAYS
OF THE
MOUNT HOOD REGION

OREGON
NATIONAL FOREST
OREGON

United States Department of Agriculture

Contribution of the
Forest Service

William B. Greeley - Forester

UNITED STATES DEPARTMENT OF AGRICULTURE
DEPARTMENT CIRCULAR 105

Contribution from the Forest Service
WILLIAM B. GREELEY, Forester

Forest Trails and Highways of the Mount Hood Region

On the mountain roads near the summit of the Cascades

Automobile Highways Through the Scenic Mountain Regions of Northwestern Oregon.

IN the Mount Hood region, a few miles from Portland, the traveler finds himself in outdoor surroundings of that primitive and youthful freshness which inspired Bryant to write of "* * * the continuous woods, where rolls the Oregon and hears no sound save his own dashings." The wild natural beauty of the Columbia River Gorge, so largely untouched, brings to mind the spirit of the days when the great river indeed knew no sound save the shouts of Indians and the songs of the voyageurs. Not so very many years ago this entire region was a vast and unbroken wilderness; and to-day the autoist speeds past rapids and portages as picturesque now as in the days when they were toilsomely negotiated by the pioneers.

The two principal routes of automobile travel in the Mount Hood region are the Columbia River highway and the Mount Hood loop road. The Columbia River highway follows the south bank of the river through the famous Columbia River Gorge, which has made the highway one of the most beautiful mountain drives in the world. In addition, the highway is one of the best hard-surfaced automobile roads ever built, extending eastward from Portland toward Hood River for 66 miles. The hard-surfaced portion is practically completed now as far as Hood River and is being pushed steadily eastward.

Leaving Portland over the Mount Hood loop road, the tourist soon passes the outskirts of the city and the valley farm lands to climb over mountain roads to the summit of the Cascade Range, a few miles south of the pinnacle of Mount Hood. Until 1846 the only entry into the Oregon country was by sea or through the Columbia River Gorge. In 1846 what is now called the old Barlow road was opened across the Cascade Mountains, and the general route of this old road is followed by the Mount Hood loop road. The Barlow road was originally a toll road, but since 1919 it has been open for travel without toll.

The drive along the Sandy and Zig Zag River roads on the Mount Hood loop route is certain to be enjoyed by every lover of the out-of-doors. The country traversed is ever-changing in character and interest, from the low valley farms near Portland to the alpine meadow lands and forest parks of the Cascade summit. There is fishing in the streams, and delightful forest camp grounds are found along the way. Several mountain resorts are reached over this road. Government Camp, near the summit of the Cascases, is the usual starting point for the south side climbs of Mount Hood.

A pleasing side trip on the Mount Hood loop road is to follow the north bank of the Sandy River over the Devil's Backbone, passing the Marmot post office and the Aschoff Mountain Home and crossing the Sandy River about 2 miles below Brightwood, returning to the Mount Hood loop road along the south bank of the Sandy River. To make this side trip, turn to the left less than half a mile beyond the town of Sandy, going to Bull Run.

The Mount Hood loop road is hard surfaced from Portland as far as Gresham. From Gresham to the Multnomah County line there is first-class macadam road; from the county line to Sandy the road surface is good hard gravel. South and east of Sandy the route is over plank and dirt roads. Automobiles can cross the Cascade Mountains during the summer months going to Wapinitia. The trip, however, calls for careful and expert driving. Government Camp is the usual limit of automobile travel on the west side of the Cascades. Autoists with camping outfits can go as far as Frog Lake and Clear Lake on the summit of the Cascade Range.

From Hood River, on the Columbia River highway, south through the Hood River Valley toward Mount Hood, the tourist leaves the highway and travels over county roads connecting Hood River, Tucker's Bridge, Odell, Middle Val-

A mountain stream on the Columbia River highway

Witching Multnomah Falls seen from Columbia River highway

ley Mill, Mount Hood post office, Woodworth, Parkdale, Mount Hood Lodge, and Cloud Cap Inn. Some automobiles go as far south as Tilly Jane Creek and Sand Canyon, several miles south of Mount Hood Lodge. These points are the limit for automobile travel in the Hood River Valley. The drives south to Mount Hood Lodge, Cloud Cap Inn, and to the head of automobile travel in the Hood River Valley are rich in points of interest. Mount Hood as seen from the highways in the upper Hood River Valley is a spectacle of supreme and commanding scenic interest, rising here, as nowhere else, high above every other feature. During the summer season automobiles easily negotiate the grade to Cloud Cap Inn, within less than 3 miles of the summit of Mount Hood, at an elevation of 5,985 feet above the sea. Mount Hood, with an elevation of 11,225 feet above sea level, is more than half climbed at Cloud Cap Inn, which is the starting point for the north side climbs of the mountain.

A new Forest Service road is being built to Lost Lake from Dee in the Hood River Valley, and will be open for travel during the season of 1920. This route from Hood River to Lost Lake connects Hood River, Tucker's Bridge, Bloucher, Winans, and Dee; thence it follows the West Fork and the Lake Fork to Lost Lake. The drive from Hood River is now being made to a point near Cedar Springs. Here the cars are parked in the woods, and the remainder of the trip is made on foot over forest trails. Inviting forest camp grounds appeal to the autoist along the way to Lost Lake. The lake itself is one of the beauty spots of the Mount Hood region. Free public camp grounds are provided by the Forest Service, and camping for the automobilist is made easy, comfortable, and safe.

Sand Canyon, south of Mount Hood Lodge, at the head of automobile travel in the upper Hood River Valley, is the starting point of forest trails which go east, south, and west. The Elk Meadows and Lookout Mountain trails are per-

High on the mountain top overlooking the Mount Hood region

haps the most interesting and beautiful forest trails in the Mount Hood region. The proposed Mount Hood loop road, now under construction from the west side of Mount Hood, will follow the southeastern slopes of Mount Hood over the country now traversed by these trails, and so in time the tour of the mountain can be made in automobiles.

The map accompanying this folder shows the important highways and mountain roads accessible to automobile travel in the Mount Hood region. Great as may be the pleasure of touring over the automobile highways of the Mount Hood region, however, the chief charm lies more often in the swift flight from the crowded city streets to the places where the forest trails begin. The traveler will miss a large part of the joy if he fails to leave his automobile for a while and go adventuring on one of these trails.

Trails of the Mount Hood Region.

Tramping over forest trails may be a new and novel experience for many, but these forest walks afford most wholesome pleasure and are safe adventures for everyone willing to learn the simple lessons of good woodsmanship. Timid ones will be amply rewarded if they venture but a few miles to glimpse a view of some waterfall hidden in a narrow cleft of the mountains and surrounded by forest; others, more bold, will follow the trails to the mountain top, where, with vision unobstructed, the eye can sweep a vast horizon of snowclad peaks and forested hills.

Charming spots in the forest, carpeted with moss and fern and roofed overhead with canopies of trees, provide camping grounds for the wanderer on the forest trails, where the peace of the woods is enhanced perhaps by the cheerful notes of a wren whose mate is nesting under a log close by. At night the hooting of an owl may boom over tree tops and hills in weird notes which startle the camper, but the murmuring water soon lulls him to sleep again. The sound of the waters is seldom lost, by night or day; for the trails seek the natural pathway cut by the streams.

The Larch Mountain Trail.

The Larch Mountain trail, the most popular forest trail in the Mount Hood region, begins on the Columbia River highway at the base of Multnomah Falls. Its prominent features are Multnomah Falls, Upper Multnomah Falls, views of the Columbia River from the canyon bluffs, and views of Mount Hood and the surrounding mountain country from the summit crag of Larch Mountain. The summit of the mountain is slightly over 6 miles from Multnomah Falls station. The ascent is gradual, over good trails the entire distance. The elevation of Larch Mountain is 4,050 feet.

The Daylight Climb.

Take the 7.30 a. m. Oregon-Washington Railroad & Navigation Co. train from Portland Union Station for Multnomah Falls. Go up the trail and over Benson Bridge, from which there is a good view of Multnomah Falls. After passing the bridge the trail to the summit of the river bluffs leads to points giving interesting views of the Columbia River. Leaving the bluffs, the trail turns back to Multnomah Creek, above the falls near the 1-mile board.

Near the 1½-mile board are two upper falls, each about 80 feet high. At about 1¾ miles the Wahkeena trail turns right, going 4 miles westerly to Wahkeena Falls and to the Columbia River highway. The Larch Mountain trail goes left, follows Multnomah Creek, and ascends.

At 2¾ miles cross the Palmer mountain road. Care must be taken to distinguish the trail from the road. Keep to the trail on the right. A sign points to the trail. Last drinking water is near the 5-mile board. There is no water at the summit of the mountain. The summit of Larch Mountain is a short distance beyond the 6-mile board. The best views are from the Forest Service fire-lookout tower and from Summit Crag.

On the Larch Mountain trail

Beautiful Mount Hood from the slopes of Larch Mountain

Returning to Columbia River highway, turn left near the 2-mile board, going over the Wahkeena trail to Wahkeena Falls, from which Columbia River highway automobile stages run to Portland.

The walk both ways is about 15 miles. It is a shorter walk (about 13 miles) returning over the same route taken going out, arriving at Multnomah Falls Station in time to take the Oregon-Washington Railroad & Navigation Co. 4.27 p. m. train returning to Portland.

The Night Climb.

Leave Portland Union Station on the 5.30 p. m. Oregon-Washington Railroad & Navigation Co. train for Multnomah Falls. Ascend trail to camp grounds near the spring close to the 5-mile board. Camp for the night at the spring. A feature of the night climb is that it enables one to enjoy the beautiful sunrise views of Mount Hood. The walk on the return trip is 9 miles by way of Wahkeena Falls or 7 miles by way of Multnomah Falls station.

The night climb is recommended for all those who enjoy sleeping outdoors for one night, and for those who do not wish to walk more than 8 or 9 miles in one day. The night trip can also be made by leaving Portland on the 11 p. m. Oregon-Washington Railroad & Navigation train, arriving at Multnomah Falls near midnight, and climbing to the spring in time for an early breakfast; then proceeding to the summit before sunrise. This schedule is very popular with Portland outing clubs.

The Wauna Point Trail.

The Wauna Point Trail is a short trail leading to a high commanding point of view about 5½ miles from the Columbia River highway, overlooking the Columbia River. This trail is accessible to the popular Eagle Creek camp grounds, and is a trip very conveniently taken by automobile campers at Eagle Creek or from Bonneville by those who leave Portland by train. The round trip walk is about 12 miles.

Schedule of Trip.

Leave Portland Union Station on the 7.30 a. m. Oregon-Washington Railroad & Navigation train for Bonneville. Detrain and visit the Oregon State fish hatchery. Leaving the fish hatchery, walk over the Columbia River highway to the beginning of the Wauna Point trail and climb through very pleasant woods to the summit of the Columbia River bluffs on Wauna Point, elevation about 2,200 feet. Wauna Point overlooks the Columbia River and Eagle Creek. Returning, descend to the Columbia River highway and go to Eagle Creek camp grounds. There take the 4 p. m. automobile stage over the Columbia River highway to Portland, or the 4 p. m. Oregon-Washington Railroad & Navigation train returning to Portland from the Eagle Creek flag station.

There is a Forest Service registering booth on the summit of Wauna Point. Visitors are requested to register their names. The last drinking water is near the 5-mile board. This is the best short trail trip from Bonneville and the Eagle Creek camp grounds.

The Eagle Creek and Herman Creek Trail.

The Eagle Creek trail is one of the costliest and best mountain trails in the West. For thousands of feet it has been cut through solid rock, and in one place goes behind a waterfall through a tunnel cut into the mountain. The trip to Wahtum Lake over the Eagle Creek trail, returning over the Herman Creek trail, requires two days' time. The distance to Wahtum Lake over the Eagle Creek trail is 13½ miles. Returning to the Columbia River highway over the Herman Creek trail the distance is 11 miles.

Schedule of Trip.

Take the 7.30 a. m. Oregon-Washington Railroad & Navigation train from Portland Union Station for Eagle Creek. The conductor must be requested to stop the train at Eagle Creek flag station.

From Eagle Creek station follow the trail to the Columbia River highway and Eagle Creek camp grounds. Ascend the trail on the left bank of Eagle Creek.

Points of interest on the Eagle Creek trail are Metlako Falls, 2 miles; Punchbowl Falls, 2½ miles; High Bridge and Canyon, 3½ miles; and Tunnel Falls, 6½ miles. Walk to Camp Shelters, 4½ miles, where noon lunch may be eaten. The distance from this point to Wahtum Lake is 9 miles.

Arrival at Wahtum Lake will be early in the evening. Meals can sometimes be obtained at the Wahtum Lake Boy Scout lodge. Camp for the night on free Forest Service camp grounds and in Forest Service camp shelters on the south

shore of the lake. To return to the Columbia River highway, go east and north around the shores of Wathum Lake over the Herman Creek trail, which begins near the camp shelters at Wahtum Lake. The distance to the highway over this route is slightly less than the distance over the Eagle Creek trail. The Herman Creek trail goes to the Herman Creek Ranger Station on the Columbia River highway, where the 3.30 p. m. automobile stages over the highway can be taken to Portland, or one may walk to Cascade Locks and return to Portland on the 3.50 p. m. Oregon-Washington Railroad & Navigation train.

Wahtum Lake is a beautiful small body of water, about half a mile long and not quite so wide, surrounded entirely by forested slopes untouched by forest fires. Excellent trails go

Looking toward Wauna Point on the Eagle Creek trail

entirely around the lake and reach all of the most interesting points of view. One trail climbs almost to the summit of Mount Chinidere, near the lake, going to the base of the cliffs within a few hundred feet of the summit. Another trail goes south 4 miles to Indian Mountain, where there is a Forest Service fire lookout station. The lake is a deep mountain lake fed entirely by springs. It has been stocked with eastern brook trout, and fair catches are made. The Portland Boy Scouts of America have built a large log-cabin lodge at Wahtum Lake and establish a summer camp there each season.

The best observation points are Mount Chinidere and Indian Mountain. Five snow-clad peaks are visible from Mount Chinidere—Mount Rainier, Mount Adams, Mount St. Helens, Mount Hood, and Mount Jefferson. In many respects, particularly to the north of the Columbia River, the view from Mount Chinidere is better than that from Indian Mountain, even though the latter peak is slightly higher in elevation. There are many interesting points of view on the way to Indian Mountain along the ridge-line trail leading to the fire-lookout station on the summit. The view from the summit of Indian Mountain itself is one that has commended its use as a fire-lookout point by the Forest Service. An observer is stationed here all summer, ever on the lookout for the telltale smoke which indicates a forest fire. Visitors to the lookout station are always welcome, and the observer will gladly furnish information of the country seen from the station tower.

The Columbia River gorge

Table of distances by shortest route between points. Oregon National Forest (see map).

From—To	Port- land.	Esta- cada.	Hood River.	Gov- ern- ment Camp.	Wapi- nitia.	Park- dale.	Cas- cade Locks.
	Miles.	Miles.	Miles.	Miles.	Miles.	Miles.	Miles.
Austin Hot Springs	71	38	..	44	53	..	..
Brooks Meadow	..	..	29	..	..	16	..
Bull Run	25	..	..	..	..	..	..
Cascade Locks	46	57	20	..	89	40	..
Chinidere Mountain	60	..	..	..	..	..	..
Clackamas Lake	75	62	..	20	33	47	..
Clear Lake	67	54	..	12	28	..	..
Cloud Cap Inn	96	..	31	13	..	11	51
Dulur	105	..	39	68	30	59	..
Elk Meadow	100	..	34	12	..	14	..
Estacada	35	..	77	42	80	97	57
Eagle Creek Camps	44	..	23	..	89	43	3
Gresham	14	21	56	41	79	76	36
Government Camp	55	42	47	..	38	27	..
Hood River	66	77	..	47	69	20	20
Indian Mountain	62	..	..	..	..	..	..
Lookout Mountain	..	..	36	29	30	23	..
Lost Lake	91	..	25	..	..	20	..
Larch Mountain	39	50	41	..	..	..	..
Marmot	32	..	..	..	..	..	..
Mount Hood Summit	63	50	36	8	43	16	56
Mount Hood Lodge	91	..	25	22	..	5	45
Multnomah Falls	32	43	34	..	..	54	14
Oregon City	16	20	52	87	..	..	..
Parkdale	86	..	..	..	..	..	..
Portland	..	35	66	55	90	86	46
Rhododendron	46	..	..	..	..	..	46
Sandy	25	12	66	30	65	..	46
Squaw Mountain	49	18	..	29	54	..	..
Still Creek and Zig Zag Summer Home areas	45	..	..	..	..	..	..
The Dalles	90	87	24	80	45	44	44
Tygh Valley	120	67	54	50	15	..	74
Wahtum Lake	58	..	..	..	..	..	14
Wapinitia	90	42	69	38	..	..	..
Welches	43	30	..	15	50	..	..

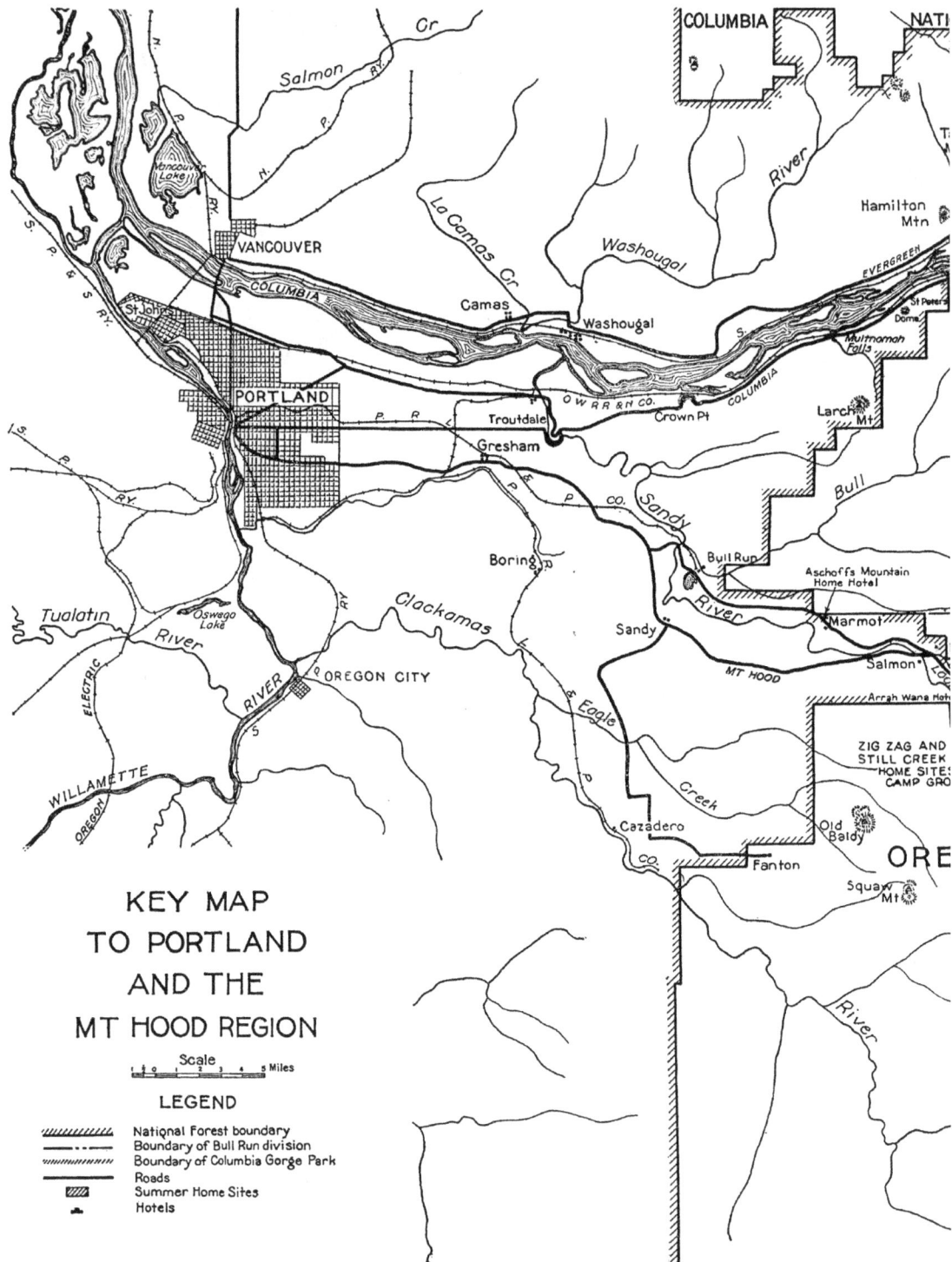

KEY MAP
TO PORTLAND
AND THE
MT HOOD REGION

Scale

1 ½ 0 1 2 3 4 5 Miles

LEGEND

////////	National Forest boundary
— · · — · · —	Boundary of Bull Run division
////////	Boundary of Columbia Gorge Park
————	Roads
▨	Summer Home Sites
▬	Hotels

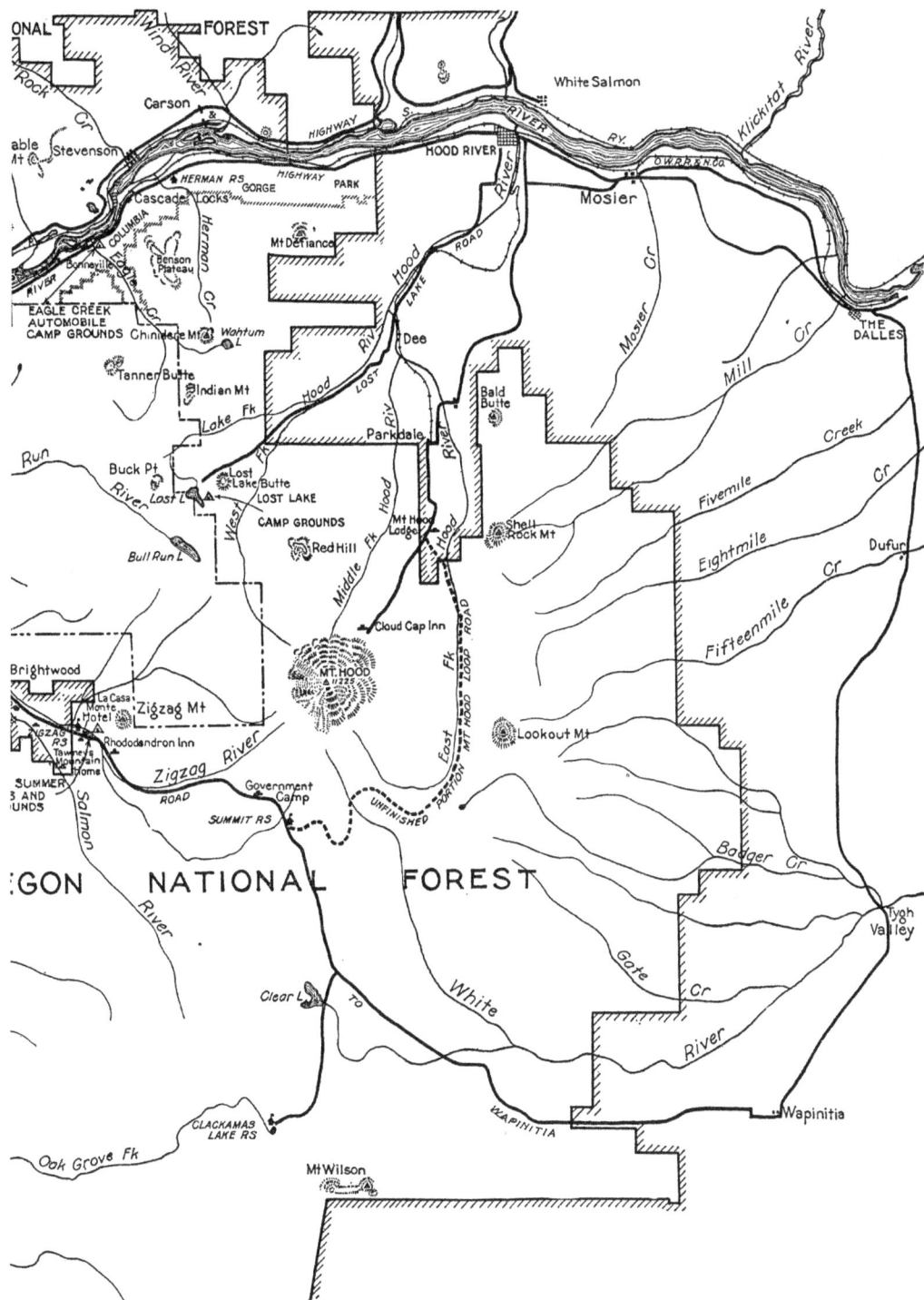

Miles.   *Features of the trail.*

0.0 The Eagle Creek camp grounds. Entrance to the camp grounds is on the Columbia River highway east of the Eagle Creek Bridge. On right hand macadam road, follow Eagle Creek. Automobile parking area of left; public-comfort station east of parking area.

0.1 On macadam road, descend to banks of Eagle Creek. Picnic tables, spring water, camp-fire cooking places, and free firewood are on the right of road beneath alder trees along Eagle Creek. Foot-bridge turns right across Eagle Creek to camp grounds on opposite banks. Forest Service registering booth is near the footbridge on the right of road.

PLEASE REGISTER HERE.

0.2 On macadam road, through park of large fir trees on the banks of Eagle Creek. Picnic tables, spring water, camp-fire cooking places, and free firewood along road under trees. Road turns left returning to exit of camp grounds on Columbia River highway. Beginning of Eagle Creek Trail at turn of road. Follow trail along banks of Eagle Creek. A sign on left of trail reads:

METLAKO FALLS	2	miles.
PUNCHBOWL FALLS	2½	miles.
HIGH BRIDGE	4	miles.
EAGLE CREEK TUNNEL	6½	miles.
WAHTUM LAKE	12	miles.
INDIAN MOUNTAIN	15	miles.

0.4 Log jam on right of trail in Eagle Creek. Water-supply main of the Eagle Creek camp grounds crosses Eagle Creek below the log jam. Public-comfort station on left of trail, a short distance beyond log jam, in grove of alders and maples. Picnic tables, camp-fire cooking places, and spring water along trail among alders, firs, and maples.

Miles.   *Features of the trail.*

0.5 Mile board on right of trail reads:

COLUMBIA RIVER HIGHWAY, ½ MILE.

End of camp grounds. Trail follows open hillside along high cliffs and begins gradual ascent. Eagle Creek on right.

0.6 Small camp site is on island to right. Cross over to camp site on rocks in creek bed. Trail leaves open hillside, turning left into pleasant timber.

1.0 Mile board on right reads:

COLUMBIA RIVER HIGHWAY, 1 MILE.

Trail continues through fir forest.

1.1 Small spring on left of trail. Drinking water trickles into cavity in rocks. Beyond spring trail goes around rocky point and approaches high basalt cliffs. Trail ascends face of cliffs, cut into solid rocks. Iron hand rails attached to rocks.

1.3 End of ascent along cliffs. View of Eagle Creek gorge lava flows and cliffs. Creek flows into Eagle Creek on right.

1.5 Mile board on right reads:

COLUMBIA RIVER HIGHWAY, 1½ MILES.

The Devil's Stairway to Eagle Creek descends through narrow cleft in rocks on right.

1.6 Trail skirts summit of high cliffs 300 feet above Eagle Creek. Iron rails attached to rocks. Open views of Eagle Creek Gorge and Summit of ridge west of Eagle Creek.

2.0 Short distance before 2 miles a sign board on right reads:

METLAKO FALLS.

Short foot trail turns right in direction of sign board to view point of Metlako Falls, height 108 feet. Spring to left of view point trail in rocks. Short distance beyond view point trail a mile board reads:

COLUMBIA RIVER HIGHWAY, 2 MILES.

2.2. Trail goes left and crosses creek. Drinking water.

2.5. A mile board reads:

COLUMBIA RIVER HIGHWAY, 2½ MILES.

Punchbowl Falls. A signboard reads:

HIGHBRIDGE, 1½ MILES.
EAGLE CREEK TUNNEL, 4 MILES.

Foot trail turns right to views of Punchbowl Falls and down into gorge below the Punchbowl.

2.6. Trail crosses creek on short log bridge. Falls below bridge. Camp and lunch site on left of trail at bridge. Build camp fires and burn lunch refuse in rock fireplace provided. Foot trail turns right near bridge to view point above Punchbowl Falls and to camp sites on Eagle Creek above the falls.

2.7. Trail crosses open rock slide.

2.9. Through open brushy timber on rocky hillside entering parklike timber.

3.0. Mile board reads:

COLUMBIA RIVER HIGHWAY, 3 MILES.

Trail goes along summit of high cliffs.

3.1. Trail enters narrow canyon of creek on left. Crosses a narrow rock gorge over a high log bridge supported by one log pillar.

3.3. Trail crosses a rock slide—"The Singing Stones."

3.5. A mile board reads:

COLUMBIA RIVER HIGHWAY, 3½ MILES.

3.7. A beautiful small waterfall is seen on opposite banks of Eagle Creek.

3.8. Trail enters a deep rocky gorge clinging to the face of a high perpendicular rock cliff, on the edge of a cleft in the rocks, less than 25 feet wide and 125 feet deep. Eagle Creek below. A spring and drinking water is on right of trail near high log bridge crossing the chasm. Trail goes over bridge.

3.9. Trail continues through fir timber on right bank of Eagle Creek with views of High Bridge and Eagle Creek gorge.

4.0. Mile board on right reads:

COLUMBIA RIVER HIGHWAY, 4 MILES.

Rainbow Falls on left.

4.3. Sheltered hollow in Eagle Creek gorge. Free public camping grounds on left after crossing bridge. Creek and falls on left.

4.4. Trail leaves camp grounds and follows face of rock cliffs into the Eagle Creek burn. Forest shows marked signs of destruction by forest fire. Creek flows into Eagle Creek on right.

4.5. Mile board on right reads:

COLUMBIA RIVER HIGHWAY, 4½ MILES.

4.6. Creek flows into Eagle Creek on right.

5.0. Mile board reads:

COLUMBIA RIVER HIGHWAY, 5 MILES.

5.3. Trail crosses small stream over bridge. High waterfall above trail on left.

5.5. Mile board on right reads:

COLUMBIA RIVER HIGHWAY, 5½ MILES.

Trail passes through open valley with free views of the surrounding ridges.

5.7. Small creek flows into Eagle Creek on right.

5.9. Small creek flows into Eagle Creek on right.

6.0. Mile board reads:

COLUMBIA RIVER HIGHWAY, 6 MILES.

6.1. Trail crosses a long rock slide. High cliffs and steep mountain sides on both sides of Eagle Creek.

6.2. Trail passes underneath high rock cliffs. Waterfalls on right. Trail is cut through massive columnar basalt, a volcanic lava-rock formation of prismatic columns. Trail now enters a rocky narrows with three high waterfalls.

6.3. Approaching Eagle Creek Tunnel. The trail is cut into the perpendicular rock wall of the cliff and goes behind a high waterfall through a tunnel cut into solid rock.

6.5. Mile board reads:

COLUMBIA RIVER HIGHWAY, 6½ MILES.

Trail follows high rock cliffs and ascends to summit of waterfalls on Eagle Creek. The valley of Eagle Creek widens and opens above the falls.

6.8. Trail skirts rock cliff. Waterfalls on right.

7.0. Mile board reads:

COLUMBIA RIVER HIGHWAY, 7 MILES.

7.4. Two camp shelters on banks of Eagle Creek, in open burn. Trail crosses two small streams beyond camp shelters.

7.5. Mile board reads:

COLUMBIA RIVER HIGHWAY, 7½ MILES.

7.9. Trail turns left and leaves Eagle Creek, ascending mountain toward Wahtum Lake.

8.0. Mile board reads:

COLUMBIA RIVER HIGHWAY, 8 MILES.

8.2. Small stream crosses trail.

8.5. Mile board reads:

COLUMBIA RIVER HIGHWAY, 8½ MILES.

8.6. Small stream crosses trail shaded by small grove of alder trees. Trail ascends open burned-over mountain side.

9.0. Mile board reads:

COLUMBIA RIVER HIGHWAY, 9 MILES.

9.5. Mile board reads:

COLUMBIA RIVER HIGHWAY, 9½ MILES.

9.6. Trail turns right around a high observation point with excellent views of Eagle Creek Valley and surrounding mountains.

9.7. Trail enters green forest.

10.0. Mile board in green timber reads:

COLUMBIA RIVER HIGHWAY, 10 MILES.

10.2. Trail winds through pleasant timbered ravine. Two small streams cross trail. Drinking water.

10.5. Mile board reads:

COLUMBIA RIVER HIGHWAY, 10½ MILES.

11.0. Mile board reads:

COLUMBIA RIVER HIGHWAY, 11 MILES.

11.3. Trail crosses small stream in a narrow timbered ravine.

11.5. Mile board reads:

COLUMBIA RIVER HIGHWAY, 11¼ MILES.

11.7. Two small streams cross trail. Trail goes through open timber on rocky mountain sides.

12.0. Mile board reads:

COLUMBIA RIVER HIGHWAY, 12 MILES.

12.1. Trail enters beautiful forest grove after crossing mountain stream on bridge. Two camp shelters and free public camp grounds on left of trail.

12.5. Mile board reads:

COLUMBIA RIVER HIGHWAY, 12½ MILES.

13.0. Mile board reads:

COLUMBIA RIVER HIGHWAY, 13 MILES.

13.3. A trail turns left, crossing outlet of Wahtum Lake and goes to Camp Chinidere and Boy Scout Lodge and the shores of Wahtum Lake. Trail to Wahtum Lake goes right through virgin forest. The lake is visible on left.

13.5. Mile board reads:

COLUMBIA RIVER HIGHWAY, 13½ MILES.

Signboard reads:

HERMAN CREEK TRAIL (East).
EAGLE CREEK TRAIL (West).

Two camp shelters and a free public camp grounds on right of trail. A trail turns right to Indian Mountain and Lost Lake between the camp shelters.

13.7. The old Herman Creek trail turns right going to summit of ridge. New trail goes left around shores of Wahtum Lake, ascending slopes to Chinidere Mountain.

14.9. New Herman Creek trail turns right. Trail to Mount Chinidere and Benson Flat goes left.

15.3. Trail ascends to edge of timber on rock slide on south slopes of Mount Chinidere. Leave trail and ascend right rocky slopes to climb Mount Chinidere. Climb to summit about 5 minutes. Mountain peaks visible from summit of Mount Chinidere: Mount Hood, Mount Jefferson, Mount Adams, Mount St. Helens, Mount Rainier; lesser peaks, Indian Mount, Mount Defiance, Larch Mount.

A forest trail on the shores of Wahtum Lake

Wahtum Lake

Boy Scout lodge and camp at Wahtum Lake

The Lost Lake Trail.

Lost Lake, reached over the Dee-Lost Lake trail, is the most beautiful mountain lake in the Mount Hood region, and is visited every year by hundreds of people. The lake is famous for the views of Mount Hood which are obtained from the northwest shores. The water is crystal clear, fed in part by springs and in part by small streams which spring from the surrounding hillsides. The chief attractions are fishing, swimming, and forest walks around the lake and over the surrounding forest trails. The lake has been stocked with trout, and fishing is good. The water warms considerably during the summer months, and since no glacial streams or snow water flow into the lake the summer temperature of its waters is admirably adapted to swimming and water sports. Many local residents from Hood River Valley visit Lost Lake every summer during the berry season to pick the huckleberries which grow on the neighboring mountains. A forest ranger is stationed at the lake during the summer months.

Schedule of the Trip.

Leave Portland Union Station on the 7.30 a. m. Oregon-Washington Railroad & Navigation train to Hood River; change to the Mount Hood Railway stage to Dee. From Dee the walk to the lake is about 14 miles. Good camp grounds are situated about 7 miles from Dee on the Dee-Lost Lake road. Vigorous hikers will make the trip to Lost Lake the same day. Automobile transportation may be secured for the trip from Dee to Cedar Springs, within 4 miles of the lake. The best camp grounds on the shores of the lake are found near the north and east end of the lake, where the trail comes down to the water's edge. The cabin of the forest ranger can be seen in a southwesterly direction across the lake. A foot trail goes west around the north and west shores to the cabin.

For the return trip the railway stages over the Mount Hood Railway leave Dee for Hood River daily at 1 p. m. Good walkers can make the entire distance in the morning; others may have

Forest ranger's cabin on Lost Lake

Lost Lake

Boating on Lost Lake

to camp out along the trail. Another return route is over forest trails to Wahtum Lake and then over the Eagle Creek or the Herman Creek trail to the Columbia River highway. This route should only be attempted by the most vigorous and hardy walkers. The distance to Wahtum Lake from Lost Lake is about 12 miles; to the highway it is about 25 miles.

The Elk Meadows and Lookout Mountain Trail.

One of the most scenic mountain trails of the region is that to Elk Meadows and Lookout Mountain. At least three days (preferably four) are required to make this journey from Portland. Elk Meadows, within sight of the glaciers, is one of the most beautiful mountain-meadow camp grounds on the slopes of Mount Hood, while Lookout Mountain is one of the best view points in the State of Oregon, commanding a view of 10 snow-clad peaks of the Cascade Range—Mount Rainier, Mount Adams, Mount St. Helens, Mount Hood, Mount Jefferson, Mount Washington, Three Fingered Jack, and the Three Sisters.

Schedule of Four-day Trip.

Leave Portland Union Station on the 7.30 a. m. Oregon-Washington Railroad & Navigation train for Hood River. Take the Mount Hood Railway to Parkdale, or automobile stages to Mount Hood lodge. Go to Sand Canyon in a light automobile hired for the occasion. The distance from Sand Canyon to Elk Meadows is about 7 miles by trail. Camp at Elk Meadows the first night. From Elk Meadows go south over a good trail to Bennett Pass, about 7 miles; thence east and north over ridge-line trails to High Prairie on Lookout Mountain, about 8 miles. Camp at High Prairie the second night. The elevation of Lookout Mountain is 6,540 feet. High Prairie is about 300 feet lower. A feature of this trail trip is an early

morning climb to the summit of Lookout Mountain to obtain sunrise views of the Cascade Range and eastern Oregon.

Returning from Lookout Mountain, go over trails to Brooks Meadows, following the summit of the mountain ridge; thence along the ridge to Rim Rock and Long Prairie. Camp there for the night, or descend westerly over trail to Mount Hood post office, 7 miles, and stay overnight at Everson's Ranch. In the morning, walk to Woodworth, take the Mount Hood Railway morning train to Hood River, and return to Portland from Hood River in the morning or early afternoon on the Oregon-Washington Railroad & Navigation train. If camp is made near Rim Rock or at Long Prairie, considerable time can be spent at Rim Rock, where the best views of Mount Hood and the Upper Hood River Valley are obtained, and the descent to Mount Hood post office and Woodworth made in time to take the 1 p. m. Mount Hood Railway train to Hood River and from there a late afternoon Oregon-Washington Railroad & Navigation train, arriving in Portland in the evening.

Schedule for Three-day Trip.

Leave Portland Union Station on the 7.30 a. m. Oregon-Washington Railroad & Navigation train for Hood River. Take Mount Hood Railway train for Parkdale, arriving about noon. Go from Parkdale to Sand Canyon in a light automobile hired for the trip. Walk easterly from Sand Canyon over forest trail, ascending mountains to Brooks Meadows, 5 miles; thence turn north from Brooks Meadows over ridge-line trail and go to camp site at Cold Spring near Mill Creek buttes and Shell Rock Mountain, and camp the first night.

Excellent sunset and sunrise views can be had from Shell Rock Mountain and Mill Creek buttes. Mill Creek buttes are the easiest observation points to climb from the camp site. In the morning proceed northerly over ridge-line trails

Mount Hood from Elk meadows

to Rim Rock and Long Prairie. From Long Prairie descend westerly over trails to Mount Hood post office, and spend the second night there. Take the early morning Mount Hood Railway train to Hood River, and return to Portland from Hood River on the morning Oregon-Washington Railroad & Navigation train, arriving Union Station, Portland, near noon of the third day. The return trip to Portland from Hood River may be taken over the Columbia River highway. The Hood River Valley stages connect with the Columbia River highway stages. Stage fare over the Columbia River highway is only slightly more than railroad fare.

The time given for the trips scheduled over the Elk Meadows and Lookout Mountain trail does not permit many stops along the way. The three-day schedule does not take the traveler either to Elk Meadows or Lookout Mountain, but only over the most scenic portion of the ridge-line trail. At least one week—if possible, two weeks—should be allowed to take the Elk Meadows and Lookout Mountain trail trip, as there are many places along the way where the traveler may wish to make a detour from the trail for a short time in order to climb to a pinnacle of rock for the view or to explore the shores of a mountain lake or an inviting section of forest. The Elk Meadows and Lookout Mountain trip is recommended to all those who wish to spend from one to two weeks journeying in the woods.

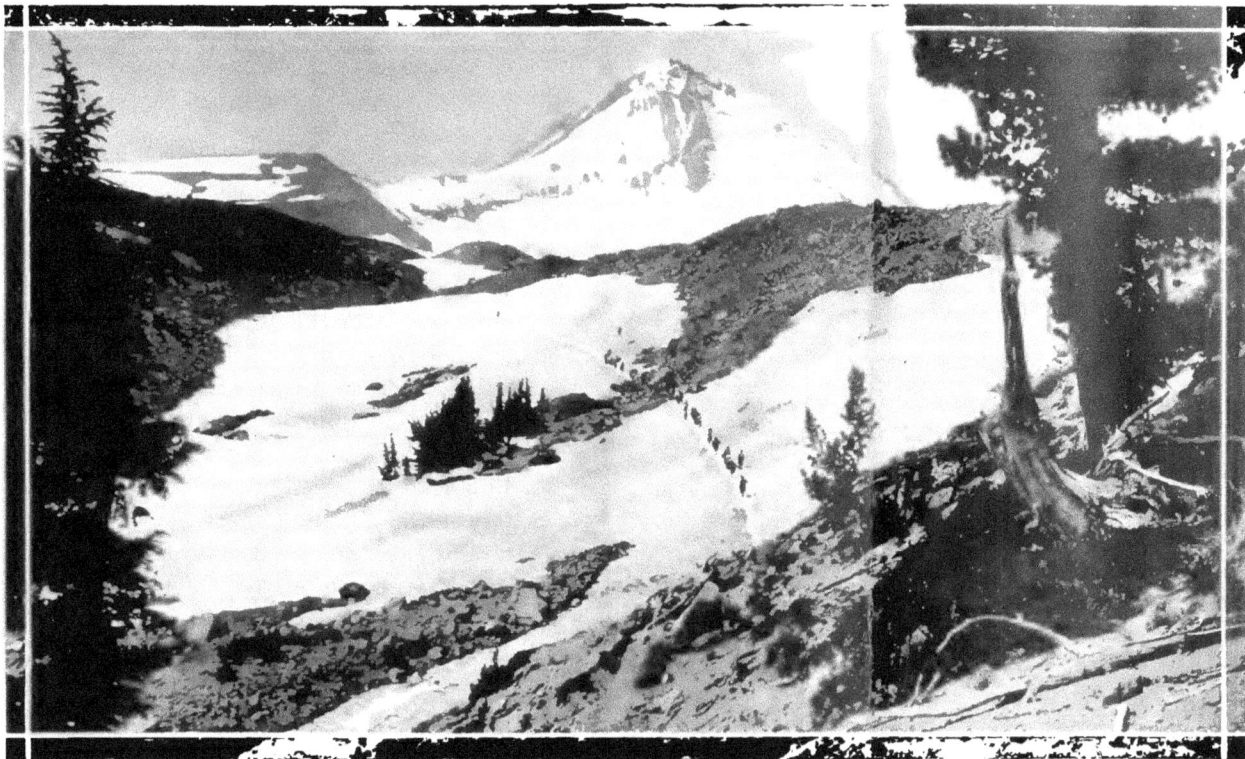

The North Side trail to the summit from Cloud Cap Inn

The North-side Climb of Mount Hood.

The north-side climb of Mount Hood is made from Cloud Cap Inn, where climbing parties are organized during the season by competent mountain guides. Inexperienced persons should not attempt to climb Mount Hood without a guide. The ascent from the north side is the most difficult, and will appeal most to lovers of mountain climbing. Parties of men and women climbers, however, have climbed the mountain from the north side and no exceptional difficulties are encountered. The views of the mountain obtained from the Hood River Valley side are quite different from those of the south side, the cone shape of the mountain being much more distinct on the north side than on the south,

as a result of differences in erosion and in exposure to the sun and the melting ice and snows.

Mount Hood is climbed annually by large numbers of people. Mountain-climbing clubs of Portland make the ascent frequently with parties numbering as high as 100 people or more. The Forest Service has established a forest-fire lookout station on the summit, where experienced observers are stationed during the entire summer fire season. Visitors are always welcome at the small building on the summit of the snow-clad peak, and many climbers have found shelter there from the biting winds which sometimes blow across the crest of the mountain. Communication with the Portland, Oreg., headquarters of the Forest Service is maintained from the summit of Mount Hood by means of an insulated telephone wire laid across the glaciers and snows. A wireless station is also being placed on the summit, and the heliograph is used under conditions which make that instrument practical and necessary.

Schedule of Trip.

There are two means of access to Cloud Cap Inn—one by rail over the Oregon-Washington Railroad & Navigation tracks and the other by automobile stage over the Columbia River highway to Mount Hood lodge. The round trip can be made over both routes. The Oregon-Washington Railroad & Navigation train leaving Union Station, Portland, at 7.30 a. m., makes connection at Hood River with railway stages and train over the Mount Hood Railway, bringing the traveler to Parkdale, near Mount Hood lodge and Cloud Cap Inn, early in the afternoon. An evening train leaves Union Station at 5.30, but does not connect with the Mount Hood Railway stage or train, which leaves Hood River at 5 p. m. An Oregon-Washington Railroad & Navigation train leaving Union Station at 9 a. m. allows several hours' time in Hood River for connection with the 5 p. m. Mount Hood Railway stage. The Mount Hood stages leave the St. Charles Hotel at Portland in the morning about 10 o'clock, en route for Mount Hood Lodge and Cloud Cap Inn. The distance by stage is close to 100 miles.

The South-side Climb of Mount Hood.

The south-side climb of Mount Hood is made from Government Camp Hotel, where climbing parties are organized during the summer season and conducted to the summit of the mountain by competent mountain guides. The ascent from the south side is much more gradual than from the north. The south slopes of the mountain are exposed to the sun, and the erosion caused by the more rapid melting of the ice and snow has made the slopes longer and gentler than the north slopes, where the steep inclines of the original volcanic cone still prevail.

Schedule of Trip.

Government Camp Hotel, near the summit of the Cascades, is reached from Portland, Oreg., by automobile stages, which leave Portland daily at 7.30 a. m. from the corner of Second and Alder Streets. The distance by stage is about 55 miles, the route being over the Mount Hood loop road. The trip can be made by train as far as Bull Run on the Portland Railway, Light & Power Co.'s electric lines. From Bull Run the remainder of the trip can be made on foot by those who so desire, going from Bull Run to the Zig Zag and Sandy River resorts over the Devil's Backbone road, passing the Marmot post office. The first night's stop can be made at the Aschoff Mountain Home, 7 miles from Bull Run. The distance from the Aschoff Mountain Home to the Sandy and Zig

Reaching the summit on Mount Hood

Zag River hotels and resorts is about 15 miles. The second night's stop can be made there. From these resorts to Government camp on the Cascade Mountain range it is slightly more than 10 miles.

No visit to the Mount Hood region is complete without a trip to the high alpine meadow slopes and forest parks near snow line on Mount Hood. It is delightful to camp on the mountain meadow within sight and sound of the glaciers, close to a flower-bordered mountain stream fed from the melting snows; and the profusion of wild-animal and plant life on the well-watered and sunny slopes of the mountain is intensely interesting to the student of nature.

The Zig Zag Mountain Trail.

Zig Zag Mountain is the most important mountain-peak point of view in the vicinity of Rowe post office and the neighboring forest camp grounds and summer resorts. The trail to the summit of Zig Zag Mountain is not plainly marked, but the mountain can be ascended without difficulty. Beyond the Zig Zag River ranger station on the Mount Hood loop road Forest Service signboards indicate the crossing of the Zig Zag River and the beginning of the trail which makes the ascent of the mountain. The climb can be made in about three hours. The view from the summit of Zig Zag Mountain is well worth the effort, this mountain on the south of Mount Hood answering about the same purposes as Larch Mountain on the north.

Schedule of Trip.

The Zig Zag River camp grounds and mountain resorts are reached by automobile stages, which run as far as Government Camp on the Mount Hood loop road. The trail is accessible to the neighboring mountain resorts, camp grounds, and Forest Service summer-home sites close to Rowe post office and vicinity, all situated close to the Mount Hood loop road stage lines. The dis-

tance to these resorts from Portland is approximately 45 miles. The trip can be made on foot from Bull Run, the terminal station on the Portland Railway, Light & Power Co.'s electric lines, by walking from Bull Run to Marmot post office over the Devil's Backbone and stopping the first night at Aschoff's Mountain Home; then proceeding the next day to Rowe post office on the Zig Zag River, about 15 miles, and camping on the Forest Service camp grounds on Still Creek and the Zig Zag River, or staying at one of the neighboring mountain resorts.

The Squaw Mountain Trail.

An interesting trail trip may be made to the summit of Squaw Mountain, altitude 4,791 feet. The view of Mount Hood and the Cascade Range south is unusually good from the summit. Masses of rhododendron grow along the trail and are in bloom during the last weeks of May and in early June. The journey can be made over Portland Railway, Light & Power Co.'s electric lines to Cazadero, and thence by trail east to Squaw Mountain, or by auto stage to the Zig Zag River resorts, and thence by trail south to the summit. The round trip can be made going out over one route and returning over the other. The walk is about 17 miles from Estacada to Squaw Mountain; from the Zig Zag River it is slightly less than 17 miles.

Schedule of Trip.

Leave Portland on the 6.45 a. m. Portland Railway, Light & Power train from the First and Adler Street station for Cazadero. Walk over roads and trails from Cazadero to forest camp grounds near Squaw Mountain on the North Fork of the Clackamas River, about 16 miles. Go via Fanton's—an old landmark of this region. Automobiles can be obtained to go as far as Fanton's, considerably shortening the journey on foot. Camp can be made within a short distance of the summit, enabling one to obtain sunrise and sunset views. Returning from Squaw Mountain via Cazadero, take the 4.45 p. m. Portland Railway, Light & Power train going to Portland. On Sundays only during the summer months there is a 6.45 p. m. train from Cazadero to Portland. Returning from Squaw Mountain, via the Zig Zag River trail, connect with Mount Hood loop road auto stages to Portland.

Going to Squaw Mountain from the Zig Zag River, take the Mount Hood loop road auto stages which leave Portland from Second and Alder Streets at 7.30 a. m. and go to Welches, the beginning of the trail. From Welches ascend the Huckleberry Mountain trail. Camp on Forest camp grounds near Squaw Mountain. Return to Portland via either Welches or Cazadero.

Forest Trails North of the Columbia River.

Some forest trails north of the Columbia River, although not strictly within the Mount Hood region, are of such scenic interest and are so accessible to Portland that mention must be made of them. Chief of these trails are those going to the summit of Mount Hamilton and Beacon Rock, both built by Mr. William Biddle, of Portland. The two trails can be covered in one day by vigorous walkers, climbing first Hamilton Mountain and then Beacon Rock before time for the train returning to Portland.

Beacon Rock is a historic landmark on the lower Columbia River, having been noted and described by the explorers Lewis and Clark on their memorable expedition to the Pacific Northwest, as follows:

In the meadow to the right and some distance from the hills, stands a high perpendicular rock, about 800 feet high and 400 yards around the base; this we called the Beacon Rock. Just below is an Indian village of nine houses, situated between two small creeks.

The traveler to-day standing on the summit of Beacon Rock will gaze with interest on these two creeks and the broad Columbia River below.

The Hamilton Mountain trail is less than 6½ miles long and is built on a very good grade, delightfully easy to walk over, in this respect one of the best forest trails near Portland. The view from Mount Hamilton is far-reaching to the north and south, with the Columbia River Valley and the high bluffs on the south of the Columbia River forming the chief near-view features of interest.

Schedule of Trip.

Leave Portland from the North Bank depot on the 7.55 a. m. Spokane, Portland & Seattle Railway train, for Wahclellah Station. Walk east from Wahclellah Station along the railroad to the beginning of the Mount Hamilton trail at the base of Beacon Rock on the east side. Ascend the trail to the county road, cross the road, and continue over the trail to the summit of Hamilton Mountain. The trail passes the base of Rodney Falls on Hardy Creek. There is no water at the summit of the mountain, so canteens should be carried and filled at the falls or springs along the trail. Returning from the summit, descend to the beginning of the Beacon Rock trail on the county road. Ascend Beacon Rock trail to the summit of Beacon Rock and return to Wahclellah Station, connecting with the 5.25 p. m. Spokane, Portland & Seattle Railway train to Portland.

Forest Camp Grounds for the Automobilist.

The most accessible spots on the Oregon National Forest in the Mount Hood region are being improved by the Forest Service as rapidly as possible for use by the people as free public camp grounds. The Eagle Creek camp and picnic grounds, situated on the Columbia River highway, are accessible by automobile from Portland and are very popular. During the season of 1919 over 150,000 people enjoyed the camping facilities provided there by the Forest Service.

The Eagle Creek camp grounds are equipped with large numbers of well-made camp dining tables, camp-fire cooking stoves, and running water, which is piped from pure mountain streams and springs. Two comfort stations are equipped with modern sanitary conveniences. On Sundays and holidays large numbers of people come by train and in automobiles to spend the week end in forest surroundings, where practically everything has been done to make forest camping as convenient as possible. The camp grounds are 44 miles from Portland and 22 miles from Hood River over the Columbia River highway. A hard macadam road turns right from the highway east of the Eagle Creek bridge. This macadam road follows the east bank of Eagle Creek through the Eagle Creek camp grounds and makes a return loop through the forest, coming out again to the highway, descending the hill east of the automobile parking space. This automobile parking space on the camp grounds will accommodate over 500 machines, and on Sundays during the height of the season is taxed to its capacity.

The camp grounds within the road loop are used largely for picnic dinner parties. Tables are placed in the most suitable spots, shaded by large fir trees or by groves of alders growing near the cool waters of Eagle Creek. Water pipes are placed near the groups of tables, and camp cooking stoves are within convenient reach. A small camping space below and north of the Columbia River highway is provided for transient campers and automobile tourists who carry their own tents. Space for permanent summer tent camps is provided on the west bank of Eagle Creek about one-fourth mile from the highway over the Eagle Creek trail. City residents establish their summer camps in tents and live there for several weeks. Eagle Creek appeals to large numbers of people because the Forest Service has sought to protect and preserve the original natural environment, and has succeeded to a very large degree.

The Zig Zag River and Still Creek Camp Grounds.

The Zig Zag River and Still Creek camp grounds are being developed on the Mount Hood loop road about 45 miles from Portland, in an environment that is still largely in its original state of natural beauty. The camp-ground improvements are not so elaborate as on Eagle Creek. Those who wish to find a cool, shady retreat in the forest by the side of a mountain stream, however, and who are content to rely largely upon themselves for the establishment of camp comfort, will find the Zig Zag River and Still Creek camp grounds suited to their purpose. Thick groves of alder trees along the banks of the river and the creeks provide cool shade, and the beds of ferns and quantities of moss growing beneath the canopy of trees make a camp ground which is enchantingly green. There is fishing in the streams, and delightful forest walks can be taken over the neighboring forest trails.

The trail going to the summit of Zig Zag Mountain is situated close to the camp grounds. Mail and supplies can be obtained at the Rowe post office, which is only a short distance from the camp grounds. During the summer months there is stage service to the camp grounds over the Mount Hood loop road. An excellent forest trail goes south and west from Welches, climbing Huckleberry Mountain—a point of great popular interest to summer visitors. A continuation of the same trail goes to Squaw Mountain.

The Lost Lake Camp Grounds.

The forest camp grounds at Lost Lake are as yet inaccessible to automobiles. The road to the lake will soon be completed, however, and the camp grounds will be open to automobile campers Lost Lake is about 95 miles from Portland, Oreg., over the Columbia River highway to Hood River, and thence over Hood River Valley roads to Lost Lake. The road during the summer of 1919 was completed to within about 4 miles of the lake.

Summer Home Sites on the Oregon National Forest.

There are two delightful sections of forest in the Mount Hood region which have been surveyed and subdivided by the Forest Service for use by the public as building sites for the erection of permanent summer homes. Here one may lease a small but suitable building lot from the Government for a nominal rental and build his summer home. One of these summer home-site areas, the Zig Zag River area, is located along both banks of the Zig Zag River on the Mount Hood loop road, near the Rowe post office, about 45 miles from Portland, Oreg. The other area is located on the shores of beautiful Lost Lake, 95 miles from Portland, in the heart of the Cascade Mountains, within but a few miles of the snow-clad slopes of Mount Hood.

The Zig Zag River sites have the advantage of being easily accessible to Portland. With the improvement of the Mount Hoop loop road the run from Portland can be made in little more than two hours. Rowe post office, only a short distance away, offers mail service and store supplies. Daily stages from Portland pass the area. The Zig Zag River lots are laid out in a long strip along both banks of the river. Thick groves of alder trees shade the banks of the stream; and heavy beds of ferns, moss, and forest undergrowth make an ideal environment for a summer home. There is some fishing in the Zig Zag River and in the tributary streams. Forest trails lead to the surrounding mountain slopes and up the stream valleys. The distance to Government Camp near Mount Hood is about 12 miles over the Mount Hood loop road. Several mountain resorts are within a short distance of the home-site area.

Lost Lake, although soon to be opened for automobile travel, will not have regular stage service for some time. It is particularly desirable for summer homes for those who desire its mountain and forest privacy, far away from the hurried activities of the work-a-day world. The summer home-site area is located in a large section of park-like forest on the shores of the lake, on moderate slopes forested with large firs, cedars, and hemlocks, and covered with a light undergrowth of low-bush huckleberries, mingled with scattering ferns and plots of grass—a bit of wild woods delightful to walk through and explore. A sand beach on the south shore of Lost Lake is within very short walking distance of the home-site area, and a close-by stretch of high banks and deep water provides ample facilities for boat houses. On Lost Lake there are many opportunities for canoeing, boating, swimming, and other water sports.

Camp Companions.

One of the amusing and interesting phases of camp life is the part that wild animals play in it. The small chipmunk is in this respect one of the

The hand of friendship.

most interesting because of his habits and because he is so common. The chipmunk is the camper's friend in supplying amusement and entertainment, but he collects heavy toll from food supplies that are kept carelessly in camp. His habits in stealing, however, are exemplary. If there are two bars of chocolate in the camp stores which he can reach he will usually eat or carry away one before touching the other, but a pack rat will nibble at everything within reach. It is surprising, nevertheless, how great a quantity of food a small band of enterprising and diligent chipmunks can damage or carry out of camp; and so it should be remembered when making camp in the forest, miles away from a grocery, that deserted and still as the woods may appear to be, a furry band of robbers is more than likely lying in wait for booty, and everything edible had better be hung up or stowed safely away.

The robbers of camps are not all of the fur-bearing kind. The bluejay and the dull black and gray bird called the "camp robber" are frequent visitors in camp and quite able to compete with the chipmunks in many respects. Chipmunks hide their stores in small holes and burrows in the ground, under logs, sticks, and stumps. The bluejay and the camp robber hide their spoils on the tops of snags and branches. Chipmunks steal even from the bluejays and camp robbers themselves. On one occasion while the bluejays and camp robbers were carrying things away from camp and hiding them in the trees, it was observed that the chipmunks deserted the camp and all started climbing trees. The camp robbers are perhaps the least timid of any of the camp visitors, and they will take bits of bread and food from out of the hand if their familiarity is at all encouraged. They are also very bold in carrying things away from camp, taking what they can in their bills or else picking it up with their claws.

The chipmunks and the birds, with the exception of the owls, are all day workers. The mice and the rats work at night. Of these the mice will rarely be noticed. Mice sometimes store stolen grains in boots and shoes, and campers spending a night in a forest cabin may find their missing rice in their shoes in the morning.

The large wood rats, commonly called pack rats, are often the bane of the camper. These large rats delight in carrying off bright objects of metal of any sort—spoons, jewelry, tinware, and the like. The camper sleeping in a forest cabin is often awakened by these rats trying perhaps to drag a pan cover or even the pan across the floor, and making a disturbance altogether out of proportion to their size. Nothing good can be said about the pack rats. Saddles, bridles, and leather goods left lying on the ground in camp will be cut and ruined almost beyond repair. Clothing left within reach of the wood rat may be sadly inadequate for wear when discovered in the morning, and as a consequence many campers have come out of the woods wearing flour-sack and gunny-sack patches on their clothes. If there are wood rats about—and usually there are—everything in camp should be hung up out of reach at night.

Skunks are night animals particularly fond of fish, and will be attracted to camp if parts of fish or meat scraps are left unburied near by. They are absolutely harmless if undisturbed. They have been known to play about the feet of campers while feeding at night on bits of fish left from cleaning a catch of trout. Care must be taken, however, not to make a quick movement which might startle the animal, with perhaps serious consequences.

A common bird in the woods is the little brown wren, which is frequently found nesting close to camp under logs and usually near the water. The Alaska robin is also one of the common birds whose song cheers the early morning and evening hours in camp. The hoot owl is apt to remind the camper of his presence during the night. One of the most interesting birds of the region is the water ousel, or "dipper," whose cheery song is distinguished at once from all the other singers near the woodland camps.

A great deal of instructive amusement can be had in camp by observing the behavior of the camp friends of the animal world. Frequent feeding makes them quite tame, and they become very interesting camp companions. An Oregon naturalist has taken motion pictures of chipmunks in camp, attracted within range of the camera by large nuts hung on strings. These small actors of the mountain camps provided interesting entertainment for motion-picture audiences. No true lover of the out-of-doors will attempt to injure any of the harmless camp visitors in any way.

Equipment Necessary for Trail Walks.

The weather conditions in the Mount Hood region during the summer months are not severe. It is not necessary to wear heavy outing clothing unless considerable time is spent at high altitudes, and even then while exercising during the day it is advisable to wear light clothing. A common mistake is to walk and climb too heavily clothed. On the other hand, it is well to carry a few extra articles of clothing in the pack sack for use in case of storm and for wear in camp and during rest periods. Khaki clothing is excellent for summer conditions where it is necessary to scramble through underbrush and thickets. Outing clothing made out of 16 or 18 ounce wool cloth, preferably forestry cloth, serves admirably for ordinary trail travel during winter weather. If no other outing clothing is available, an old cast-off wool suit and a pair of overalls will meet the situation.

Flannel shirts are usually worn in the woods. Experience has shown that in cases of light sum-mer showers and resting after exertion flannel shirts are excellent to prevent chills. An old sweater is a great convenience in camp, can be carried easily in the pack-sack, and serves as a pillow at night. A cruiser-style overshirt, worn in place of a coat, is being manufactured on the Pacific coast and is becoming very popular with outing people. Made into a coat, this cruiser shirt answers every purpose of a man's outing coat, and it can also be modified to make a very comfortable, useful, and becoming woman's blouse.

A light home-made waterproof cape, made out of waterproofed tent silk, and weighing not more than three-quarters of a pound, is most useful to wear over the shoulders in case of rain. A very suitable cape can be made out of a rectangular piece of waterproof tent silk with a slot opening in the center for the head. This rectangular piece of cloth can be used during the night as a ground cloth for the sleeping bag or blankets and as a rain-proof cape during the day, and is very practical. The rectangle measures about 4 by 7 feet. The standard army poncho and "shelter half" are heavier, but serve the same purpose.

Any stout shoes will serve for walking over forest trails. The soles must be heavy enough to prevent stone bruises and to hold a few hobnails, which are necessary to prevent slipping on steep trails. Hobnails are also very useful to prevent slipping while walking over down timber, branches, and logs. Sharp steel calks are not necessary, except for climbing over steep, icy slopes on glaciers, or in the woods where there is much walking over logs. A steel screw calk is manufactured which can be screwed into the leather sole for wear in the woods and can be easily removed at any time. A pair of moccasins can be carried easily in the pack sack during the day, and are a great comfort to the feet in the evening in camp.

The best camp bed for the trails is made out of a pure-wool comforter sewed into a sleeping bag, and covered with an outer bag of light drill or tent silk. One 3-pound comforter is sufficiently warm for all summer conditions at low altitudes, and the combination of one additional 2-pound comforter will answer all purposes for use on mountain peaks above snow line. A light muslin lining increases the warmth of the sleeping bag, and adds greatly to its cleanliness, as this lining can be removed and washed. The lining is made by sewing a strip of muslin a yard wide and about 12 or 14 feet long into a bag to slip inside the wool-comforter sleeping bag. Sporting-goods stores supply an excellent light sleeping bag cover made out of tent silk, weighing less than 2 pounds.

The most practical shelter is a light waterproof forester's tent or a light rectangular waterproof fly weighing not more than 4 or 5 pounds. Shelter tents large enough for two persons, and which can be closed completely to shut out insect pests as well as stormy weather, can be obtained from sporting-goods stores; but these are very rarely necessary. The rectangular fly or the forester's tent are the most practical shelters under almost all conditions encountered in this region.

For camp use a light hunter's ax and a strong jackknife are necessary. Excellent camp-cooking outfits can be purchased for any sized party at sporting stores, but individuals can easily assemble their own cooking outfits by using inexpensive tinware good enough for camp use during one season. Very few dishes are necessary; the general tendency will be toward carrying too much unnecessary equipment. An excellent combination for small parties which can be obtained in the west is a set of three nesting tin pails, or two nesting pails and one nesting coffee pot. These, together with a light steel fry pan, tin cups, tin plates, knives, forks, and spoons, will serve all purposes. The army mess kit is used and liked by some campers. An army canteen is excellent for use on mountain climbs and on trails away from water.

A good compass, a waterproof matchbox, and a forest map are absolute necessities to be carried on the person at all times. A sharp knife and a supply of dry matches are indispensable on occasions too numerous to mention in the woods, and the map and compass are the constant companions of careful observers in forest and mountain regions, besides being a great factor of safety in preventing one from being lost in the woods. The map accompanying this folder is adequate for all travel on forest trails in this region.

Climbing Mount Hood.

Greater care must be taken in selecting the equipment necessary for climbing Mount Hood. Stout climbing shoes newly hobnailed and spiked with a few new and long, sharp calks are essential. Smoked glasses large enough to protect the eyes from snow glare must be worn to prevent snow blindness. Grease paints are used on the climb over the glaciers to prevent sunburn. A light pair of cheap canvas gloves will protect the hands. Alpenstocks are necessary while making the snow climb. Canteens should be carried and a handful of raw oatmeal added to the water in the canteen. A small quantity of oatmeal water quenches the thirst and has an appreciable and stimulating food quality. A large bandana handkerchief is useful as a protection from the sun. Liberal quantities of cold cream and a small hand towel are used in removing grease paint. Heavy woolen stockings should always be worn over cotton or silk. A sweater is conveniently carried in the pack sack while climbing, and is a protection against cold and chills while resting on the summit or other points on the climb. Fruit juices, fruits, and other food are carried for emergency and for refreshment on the way. If the climb is made in the company of a guide, his instructions and suggestions should always be followed. Local mountain-climbing clubs and other mountaineering associations also instruct novices who accompany their parties on climbs of Mount Hood. Inexperienced persons should not attempt the climbing of snow-clad peaks without guides or without the leadership of experienced mountaineers.

Below is a list of the clothing and equipment usually worn on the forest trails in the Mount Hood region:

1. On the person:

   Soft-felt hat or crusher.
   Cruiser coat or shirt (water-repellant duck or forestry cloth).
   Flannel shirt.
   Medium-weight cotton underwear.
   Breeches (water-repellant duck or forestry cloth).
   Heavy wool socks over silk or cotton.
   Outing boots, hobnails.
   Bandana handkerchief.
   Note book and pencil.
   Radiolite watch.
   Jackknife.
   Waterproof matchbox.
   Pocket compass.
   Camera.
   Forest guide folder and map.

2. In the pack sack:

   Forester's tent or fly.
   Waterproof cape, poncho, or shelter-half.
   Sleeping bag.
   Cooking kit.
   Food supplies.
   Camp ax.
   Pair moccasins.
   Sweater.
   Extra socks, handkerchiefs.
   Bath towel.
   Dish towel.
   Toilet articles.

All the short-trail trips described in this folder are made on foot, the necessary supplies and equipment being carried in a pack sack.

Camp equipment and supplies to last one week can be carried in a pack sack and the heaviest packs in the party should not weigh more than 60 pounds. The packs of the women members of the party should not weigh more than 35 pounds. The packs gradually become lighter as the journey approaches its close. Practically all of the longer trail journeys can be made without pack-horses or saddle horses.

Those who feel themselves to be too inexperienced or unable to lead an independent life in the woods can secure pack and saddle horses. The packer accompanying the horses will serve as guide, usually being well acquainted with the country. One pack horse will carry about 150 to 175 pounds weight. If horses are not available, men accustomed to the work of packing can sometimes be secured locally to carry the heavy pack sacks over the trails. An experienced packer can carry a pack sack of about 75 pounds. A packer able to act also as a guide and cook is a find, and worthy of his hire.

These trail descriptions give practically all of the routine information necessary for making any of the trail journeys outlined. The few suggestions on clothing and camping equipment and camping methods have been found practical in this region. The forest map shows all the roads and forest trails open for the recreation and pleasure of the public. Campers should remember also that they are not isolated in the woods while on or near the forest trails. Forest rangers and forest guards are always keeping the trails under observation, and it usually happens that their direction and help can be obtained in cases of emergency.

There is one element of danger in the public enjoyment of the mountains and forests, and that is the grave danger, imminent at all times during the summer, from forest fires. A cigarette stub, the glowing spark from an unextinguished cigar, or a carelessly thrown match may start a small fire in the woods which will soon grow to immense proportions. Hundreds of people have lost their lives, homes and forest settlements have been destroyed, and millions of acres of forest have been laid waste by forest fires which have had their beginning in carelessness with fire in or near the forest. Safety from the danger of forest fires is only possible through the carefulness and ceaseless vigilance of every individual. The carefulness of one person in the beginning is more important and effective forest-fire protection than the combined efforts of hundreds of men fighting a large forest fire. The safest protection from forest fires is habitual carefulness. The punishment of careless persons can never restore lost lives, burned forests, and the shaded greenwood trails. Everyone going into the forest is therefore cautioned to observe the following rules of good woodsmanship, and to be careful always in the use of fire:

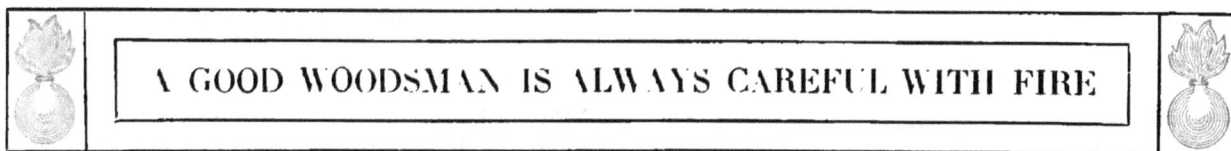

A GOOD WOODSMAN IS ALWAYS CAREFUL WITH FIRE

MATCHES.—Be sure your match is out. Break it in two before you throw it away.

SMOKERS.—Throw pipe ashes and cigar or cigarrette stubs in the dust of the road or trail and stamp them out. Do not toss cigar and cigarette stubs to the side of the car.

MAKING CAMP.—Build a small camp fire. Build it in the open, never against a tree or log. Scrape away the trash from all around it.

LEAVING CAMP.—Never leave a camp fire, even for a short time. When leaving camp extinguish every spark of it with water or dirt. Be sure that the camp fire is completely out before leaving it.

FIGHTING FIRES.—If you find a fire try to put it out. If you can't, get word at once to the nearest forest ranger or fire warden. Keep in touch with the rangers.

ALWAYS BE CAREFUL WITH FIRE
KEEP THE STREAMS PURE
KEEP A CLEAN CAMP

Take as good care of the forests as you do of your own home. Do your share in keeping them attractive. Damage to the forests means loss to everyone.

Food Supplies Suitable for the Trails.

On all trips under three days in length many standard groceries can be carried, such as fresh bread and other baked goods, package groceries, canned goods in tins or even glass, fresh meat and eggs, condensed soups, etc. On long trail trips, however, foods must be selected with care in order to keep the packs from being too heavy. Experience in the woods has proved the value of the following list of foods, and it is given for the benefit of those to whom the selection of foods for such a trail journey may be a new experience:

Foods Suitable for a Long Stay in the Woods.

Hard-tack biscuits.	Coffee.
Pea-meal biscuits.	Sugar.
Flour.	Salt.
Pancake flour.	Pepper.
Cracked wheat.	
Cereals.	Bacon.
	Butter.
Dehydrated soups.	Cheese.
Dehydrated eggs.	Fats.
Milk powder.	Oils.
Dried pitted prunes.	Beans.
Dried black figs.	Rice.
Dried apples.	Split peas.
Dried apricots.	
Raisins.	Shelled nuts.
	Peanuts.
Bar chocolate.	Almonds.
Chocolate nut bars.	Walnuts.
Malted-milk tablets.	Pecans.
	Nut butter.
Chocolate.	
Cocoa.	Condensed milk in small tins.
Tea.	

A mixture of coarsely ground whole wheat, nuts, and raisins makes a most nourishing and compact food to be carried in the woods. With thick condensed milk it is a most wholesome and appetizing dish, and can be eaten without cooking.

Rice is one of the most sustaining foods which can be taken, and can be eaten for extended periods of time without palling on the taste. Experienced woodsmen have a great preference for rice. The best quality unpolished rice should be selected.

Flour, bacon, salt, sugar, prunes, dried apples, rice, and beans are the standard necessities of the prospector, miner, hunter, and trapper.

Coffee should be ground, or some of the many brands of soluble coffees may be used.

The National Forest.

A National Forest is a large Government-owned timber farm, in charge of a forest supervisor, who may be likened to a farm superintendent, and who has for his foremen several district forest rangers, each one in charge of large subdivisions of the immense timbered domain included within the boundaries of the forest. A National Forest often contains more than a million acres—a tract of land which inclosed in a rectangle would measure about 60 miles long and almost 40 miles wide. There are 154 National Forests in the United States and Alaska.

The growing stands of timber are carefully managed by the Forest Service so as to insure the the largest possible mature timber crop perpetually to the Nation. The most important work in timber farming is to protect the growing forests from fire. On several of the high mountain peaks of the Oregon National Forest there are small lookout houses, where men are stationed at all times during the summer fire season to watch constantly over all parts of the forest for the first signs of smoke which indicate the forest fire. Telephone lines enable the observer to communicate with the district forest ranger or the forest supervisor in case a forest fire is discovered, and fire-fighting crews are dispatched at once to the scene of the fire as soon as it is reported by the

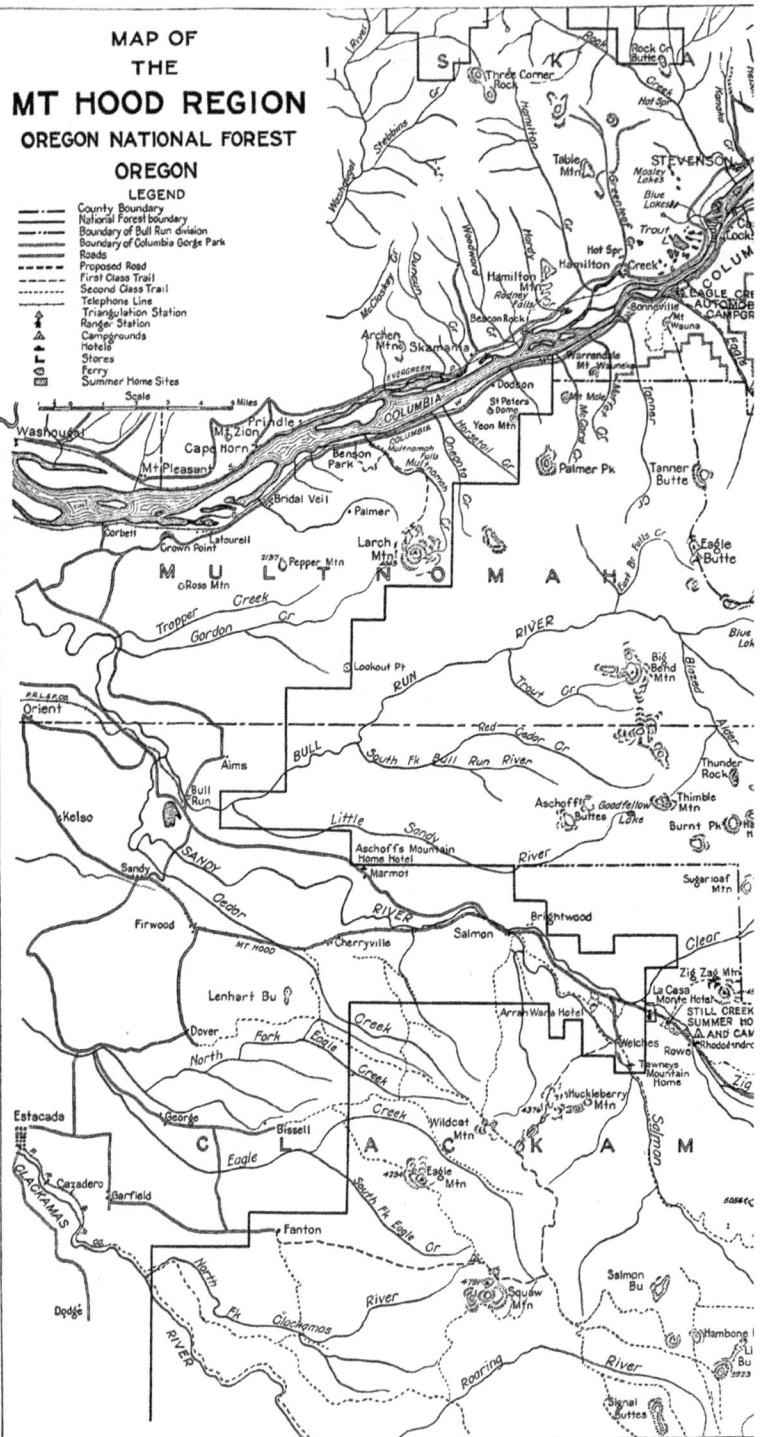

MAP OF
THE
MT HOOD REGION
OREGON NATIONAL FOREST
OREGON

LEGEND

County Boundary
National Forest boundary
Boundary of Bull Run division
Boundary of Columbia Gorge Park
Roads
Proposed Road
First Class Trail
Second Class Trail
Telephone Line
Triangulation Station
Ranger Station
Campgrounds
Hotels
Stores
Ferry
Summer Home Sites

Scale

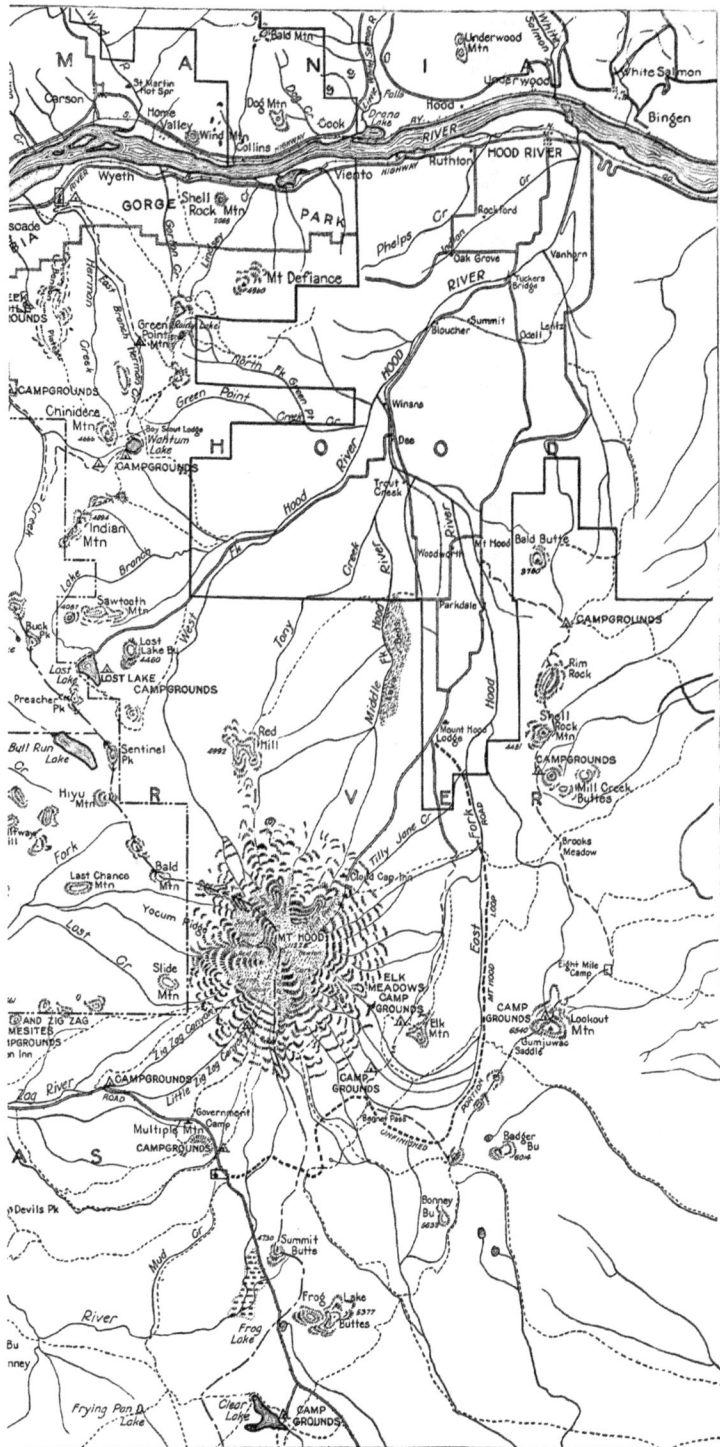

MANIA

Bald Mtn

Underwood Mtn

White Salmon

St Martin Hot Spr

Underwood

Dog Mtn

Carson

Home Valley

Wind Mtn

Collins

Cook

Drano Lake

Bingen

HOOD RIVER

Wyeth

GORGE

Viento

Ruthton

HOOD RIVER

Shell Rock Mtn

PARK

Rockford

Phelps Cr

Oak Grove

Vanhorn

Mt Defiance

RIVER

Tuckers Bridge

Summit

Sloucher

Odell

Lenz

Thirman Cr

Green Point Mtn

Winans

CAMPGROUNDS

Chinidere Mtn

Boy Scout Lodge

Wahtum Lake

Dee

HOOD

Trout Creek

CAMPGROUNDS

Indian Mtn

Woodworth

Mt Hood

Bald Butte

Parkdale

CAMPGROUNDS

Sawtooth Mtn

Buck

Rim Rock

Lost Lake B

Lost Lake

CAMPGROUNDS

Shell Rock Mtn

Preacher Pk

Red Hill

Mount Hood Lodge

CAMPGROUNDS

Bull Run Lake

Sentinel Pk

Mill Creek Buttes

Hiyu Mtn

RIVER

Brooks Meadow

Last Chance Mtn

Bald Mtn

Cloud Cap Inn

Yocum Ridge

MT HOOD

Eight Mile Camp

Slide Mtn

ELK MEADOWS CAMP GROUNDS

CAMP GROUNDS

Lookout Mtn

AND ZIG ZAG MESITES MPGROUNDS

Elk Mtn

Gumjuwac Saddle

Zig Zag River

CAMPGROUNDS

CAMP GROUNDS

Government Camp

Badger Bu

Multiple Mtn

CAMPGROUNDS

Devils Pk

Bonney Bu

Summit Butte

Mud Cr

Frog Lake

Frog Lake Buttes

River

Frying Pan Lake

Clear Lake

CAMP GROUNDS

On the Oregon National Forest

lookout men. In each lookout station there are instruments for accurately locating fires. In addition to the lookout men, the district forest ranger employs forest fire guards who patrol the forest trails during the fire season. It is their work to discover all camp fires which may have been left unextinguished, to put them out, and to arrest the careless campers.

Fire fighting is not the only work the forest ranger has to do. The district forest ranger must superintend the construction of forest roads and trails, and the building of telephone lines, bridges, and ranger-station buildings. He must administer Government sales of timber and the leasing of water-power and grazing privileges. Ripe stands of timber are selected and sold by the Government to the highest bidder. The timber is sold and marked and scaled by the forest ranger, and the timber crop is removed so as to favor as much as possible the growth of another crop of timber.

Timber is only one, however, of the many crops raised on a National Forest, although it is one of the most important. Large sections of the National Forest suitable for the grazing of cattle and sheep must be personally examined by the forest ranger. Annual permits are granted to stock owners, who are required to limit their herds and flocks to the number which the grazing areas can best carry; and such grazing rules and regulations are laid down as will best insure the restocking of the mountain pastures with grasses and forage cover for the ensuing seasons. Thus the National Forests grow annually a large crop of beef, mutton, wool, and hides.

The pure mountain water supply of many cities is drawn from the National Forests. A large portion of the Oregon National Forest is used for no other purpose than to insure a perpetual supply of pure mountain drinking water to the city of Portland. This section of the Forest is known as the Bull Run Reserve, and includes the entire watershed of the Bull Run River. The watershed is closed to the public, and no timber cutting, grazing, or other forest use is allowed. A staff of forest guards patrol the watershed district, protecting it from fire.

Electric power is also generated on many National Forests, where large areas of rocky mountain slopes, covered with heavy forest, feed mountain waterfalls which generate the electricity supplying cities with light and power.

These water-power sites on the National Forests are leased by the Government to companies. Stretches of National Forest are recognized as being chiefly valuable for outdoor recreation, and forest lands of this type are set aside to be used entirely as recreation areas. The Columbia Gorge Park division of the Oregon National Forest is forest land of this kind.

A Short Key to the Forest Trees.

In the following check list of forest trees it is purposed to describe the forest trees of this region in the fewest possible words in order to bring it within the limited space available. No attempt is made to present an elaborate key or give detailed descriptions. Its greatest use will be to give the forest traveler a few hints which will help him to identify at least some of the forest trees growing along the trails and in the forested parts of the Mount Hood region.

The pines have long needles, which are always borne in bundles, never more than five needles in a bundle. The larches have short needles in clusters or tufts, up to 30 or more needles in one cluster. The hemlocks, firs, and spruces all have short needles, which do not grow in bundles but are scattered singly along the twigs. In the case of the hemlocks the needles are soft, flat, and round at the ends and arranged only on the sides of the twig, making a flat spray; with the true firs the needles are flat and notched at the ends, and on account of a twist around the twig appear to be distributed on its upper half. In the case of the spruces the needles are stiff and sharp pointed, prickly to the touch, and distributed all around the twig.

The needles of Douglas fir, which is not true fir, are sharp pointed, but not stiff or prickly. The best way to distinguish this tree, however, is by its cones, which have peculiar three-pointed bracts or leaf-like scales protruding from between the regular scales.

The foliage of cedars is not made up of needles, but of very small leaf-scales, which clasp the twig closely. It should be stated also that although the yew is an evergreen tree with needles somewhat similar to hemlock, it is not a conifer, since it bears characteristic red berry-like fruits in place of cones.

The user of this key should keep in mind that a short description can not cover the wide variations that are bound to occur in trees of the same species due to difference in age, size, and habitat. Lengths of needles and cones may be found to vary quite considerably from the average dimensions given in this description. In all cases the descriptions here given are aimed to fit the typical mature trees. It should also be borne in mind that timber-line trees occur not only as the last outposts of tree growth where they are short and stunted, but also grow down the slopes several thousand feet lower, where they mingle with other trees and have a respectable form and size.

SOFTWOOD SPECIES.

THE CONIFERS.

Family CONIFERÆ.

PINES (PINUS).

WESTERN WHITE PINE (*Pinus monticola*).

Cylindrical trunk, clear of branches; bark (on trees over 1 foot in diameter) broken into small hexagonal blocks; needles, five in a bundle 4 inches long. Occasional tree at 1,000 to 4,000 feet elevation.

WHITE BARK PINE (*Pinus albicaulis*).

Low, long-branched, twisted, crooked trunk; needles five in a bundle 2 inches long. A timber-line tree growing on the highest timbered elevations in the Mount Hood region.

WESTERN YELLOW PINE (*Pinus ponderosa*).

Straight trunk, broad crown, heavy foliage; bark of old trees dull orange-yellow, broken into large irregular plates; needles three in a bundle 7 inches long. On the Columbia River east from Bonneville. East of the Cascades up to 5,000 feet.

LODGEPOLE PINE (*Pinus contorta*).

Small tree, occurring often in dense stands. Slender, dense-grown stems were used by the Indians for tent poles, hence the name. Thin, scaly bark, needles two in a bundle 2 inches long. North side of Mount Hood, 3,100 to 5,000 feet. On south side from Government Camp to 1,700 feet near Tollgate and at the mouth of the Sandy River.

LARCHES (LARIX).

WESTERN LARCH (*Larix occidentalis*).

Tapering trunk, open crown, foliage appears very scant. Needles 1 inch, 14 to 30 in a cluster, turn yellow and fall from tree in autumn. Only cone-bearing tree in this region which loses its leaves in the fall. On northeast and south sides of Mount Hood.

SPRUCES (PICEA).

ENGLEMANN SPRUCE (*Picea engelmanni*).

Straight, narrow, pyramidal crown; bark of trunk scaly; needles arranged singly on the twig, stiff, sharp-pointed, prickly. On Mount Hood 3,000 to 6,000 feet, Badger Lake, and Brooks Meadow.

HEMLOCKS (TSUGA).

WESTERN HEMLOCK (*Tsuga heterophylla*).

Becomes large forest tree, clean, smooth, tapering trunk. Lower foliage in delicate, flat sprays, tip of tree always bent over, terminal branchlets always drooping; needles flat, round tipped, half-inch long, dark green above, silvery underneath. Cones three-quarters inch long. Throughout the Mount Hood region up to 5,500 feet in moist situations.

MOUNTAIN HEMLOCK (*Tsuga mertensiana*).

Short alpine tree to timber line; trunk sharply tapering; needles densely clustered in star-like arrangement on the twig, not in flat sprays. Cones 2 inches long. Both slopes of the Cascade 5,500 to 7,000 feet. Timber line on Mount Hood.

DOUGLAS FIR (PSEUDOTSUGA).

DOUGLAS FIR (*Pseudotsuga taxifolia*).

The common large forest tree of this region. Thick brown bark with broad ridges and deep furrows; needles soft, pointed, but not prickly; cones about 3 inches long, with three-pointed, leaf-like scales protruding from between the cone scales. Throughout the Mount Hood region to 6,000 feet, north side of Hood to 3,800 feet, on south side up to Government Camp.

FIRS (ABIES).

ALPINE FIR (*Abies lasiocarpa*).

The common fir of the timber line. Long, narrow, conical crown, terminating in a conspicuous spirelike point. North side of Mount Hood from 3,700 feet to timber line. South side from timber line to Government Camp.

LOWLAND WHITE FIR (*Abies grandis*).

Fair-sized tree; bark ashy gray in young tree, smooth like alder bark; in old trees broken into narrow ridges and furrows. Needles broad, flat, grooved, and notched at the tip. Lustrous dark green above, silvery below. Bark of young twigs distinctly greenish yellow. Lower slopes of Mount Hood. General up to 4,000 feet.

SILVER FIR (*Abies amabilis*).

Handsome tree with conspicuously smooth light gray bark. Smooth on trees under 2 feet in diameter, broken into wide ashy plates on larger trees. North side of Mount Hood, 3,700 feet to timber line, southwest side from near Government Camp to timber line, 2,000 to 5,500 feet in the Cascades.

NOBLE FIR (*Abies nobilis*).

Magnificent forest tree. Tall and symmetrical, with a noticeably clear and straight trunk, bark broken by narrow furrows into conspicuously flat and smooth plates which are of a purplish color. North side of Mount Hood at 4,500 feet, on south side from 3 miles below Government Camp upward. Abundant on Larch Mountain, where this tree is wrongly called larch.

ARBORVITÆS (THUJA).

WESTERN RED CEDAR (*Thuja plicata*).

Large tree. Usually swell-butted, with tapering trunk and drooping branches. Thin, stringy, chocolate brown bark. Foliage not needles, but scales clasping the twigs, in flat sprays. Both sides of the Cascades, north side of Mount Hood, from 1,700 feet down to the Columbia River, on south side of Mount Hood from Government Camp to Salmon post office. Usually found in bottoms, along streams, and moist situations generally.

CEDARS (CHAMÆCYPARIS).

ALASKA CEDAR (*Chamæcyparis nootkatensis*).

Tree somewhat like western red cedar with rapidly tapering trunk, but leaf scales finer and sprays more delicate. Sprays are harsh to the touch, while those of red cedar are soft. Branches conspicuously drooping. Foliage when crushed has strong, somewhat offensive odor. On Mount Hood near Government Camp and on north side.

JUNIPERS (JUNIPERUS).

DWARF JUNIPER (*Juniperus communis*).

Always a shrub in this region. Needles very short and sharp pointed; fruit a dry, aromatic berry, blue-black when ripe. On ridge tops and summits of the Cascades. On north side of Mount Hood at 6,500 feet. Abundant on Mount Chinidere.

WESTERN JUNIPER (*Juniperus occidentalis*).

Short tree, rarely over 60 feet high, ordinarily 15 to 20 feet. East of the Cascades to 6,000 feet, on dry arid exposed places.

THE YEWS.

Family TAXACEÆ (not cone-bearing).

PACIFIC YEW (*Taxus brevifolia*).

This is the only species of yew which is native to the Northwest. Small tree, rarely 60 feet high, growing under others in the forest. Bark thin, smooth, and conspicuously purplish red; young twigs same color, green as the pointed needles. Foliage somewhat similar to hemlock, but coarser and not so droopy. Fruit bright coral-red berries ripening in September. West side of Cascades to 6,000 feet; near margins of streams and on moist flats.

HARDWOODS OR DECIDUOUS TREES.

THE WILLOWS.

Family SALICACEÆ.

WILLOWS (SALIX).

There are several species of willows in the Mount Hood region, distributed from the sand bars along the Columbia River to the headwaters and upper courses of high mountain streams, but they are so difficult to distinguish that a key to the willows can not be given, nor would it be useful in a popular description of this kind.

COTTONWOODS AND POPLARS (POPULUS).

ASPEN (*Populus tremuloides*).

Small tree, commonly 30 to 40 feet. Bark whitish, leaves small, somewhat heart-shaped, with stem flattened at base of leaf; foliage always trembling in the breeze. Usually occurs with Douglas fir, western yellow pine, and lodgepole pine east of the Cascades.

BLACK COTTONWOOD (*Populus trichocarpa*).

Large tree. Gray bark, having sharply defined ridges and furrows. Glossy large leaves turning conspicuous yellow in autumn. On both sides of the Cascades at lower levels. It is the common tree of river bottoms, sand bars, and river banks.

THE BIRCHES.

Family BETULACEÆ.

BIRCHES (BETULUS).

MOUNTAIN BIRCH (*Betulus fontinalis*).

Slender, graceful tree with deep, shiny old-copper-colored bark. Locally noted in Columbia River Valley.

ALDERS (Alnus).

White alder (*Alnus rhombifolia*).

Distinguished from red alder by having conspicuously scaly brown bark. Leaves with fine-toothed wavy borders. On eastern slopes of the Cascades in moist situation.

Mountain alder (*Alnus tenuifolia*).

Commonly with slender bent stems up to 15 feet high in dense thickets. Leaves doubly toothed, with fine teeth on the coarser teeth. On heads of mountain streams, springy slopes, borders of high meadows, and lakes.

Red alder (*Alnus oregona*.

Large alder, 60 to 90 feet high, thin smooth bark, light ashy gray. Leaves more regularly toothed and coarser than other alder trees. Undersurface of leaf coated with rust-colored hairs. Borders of streams and on moist bottoms.

THE NUT-BEARING TREES.

Family CUPULIFERÆ.

CHINQUAPINS (Castanopsis).

Western chinquapin (*Castanopsis chrysophylla*).

An evergreen, broad-leaf, shrubby tree, with thick leathery leaves, shiny green above and brownish yellow tint underneath. Fruit a nut inclosed in a burr similar to the chestnut. Valley of the Columbia River and on Mount Hood.

OAKS (Quercus).

Oregon oak (*Quercus garryana*.

A small tree, the only oak in this region. On high mountain slopes a small shrubby tree. Chiefly in the Willamette River Valley, on west slopes of Cascades to 3,000 feet, and up into lower growth of yellow pine on each side. On north and northeast slopes of Mount Hood.

THE ROSE FAMILY.

Family ROSACEÆ.

SERVICE BERRIES (Amelanchier).

Western service berry (*Amelanchier alnifolia*).

Tall, slender-stemmed shrub 8 to 10 feet high. White flowers, blue-black sweetish edible fruit. The earliest white-flowering shrub in the woods. Generally distributed.

HAWS (Cratægus).

Black haw (*Cratægus douglasii*).

Low, much-branched shrub, sometimes a tree 20 to 30 feet high. Black or black-purple, shiny, sweet, edible fruit. Branches with a few thorns, not very sharp. Foliage bright red in autumn. On borders and bottoms in vicinity of lower mountain streams.

CHERRIES AND PLUMS (Prunus).

Bitter cherry (*Prunus emarginata*).

From a slender, much-branched shrub to a tree 35 to 40 feet high. Mature fruit clear coral red, extremely bitter. In woods at lower elevations.

Western choke cherry (*Prunus demissa*).

Commonly a treelike shrub. Bruised twigs and leaves have strong scent like peach pits. Mature fruit blue-black color. Chiefly east of Cascades; on arid parts west on lowest mountain slopes.

THE MAPLES.

Family ACERACEÆ.

MAPLES (Acer).

Broadleaf maple (*Acer macrophyllum*).

Only large tree maple on Pacific coast. Mature leaves of unmistakable large size, 6 to 12 inches across. Wholly on west side of Cascades on borders of foothills and low mountain streams.

Vine maple (*Acer circinatum*).

Often of a sprawling, crooked, vinelike appearance, shrublike. Bark smooth and greenish. Leaves with seven pointed lobes which in the fall turn to brilliant red and yellow tints and form the most prominent autumn coloring of this region. Occurs very commonly.

Dwarf maple (*Acer glabrum*).

Small-stemmed shrub 4 to 6 feet high; rarely a tree. Bark smooth and red-brown with grayish cast. Leaves with three coarsely toothed lobes. Occurs but rarely.

THE BUCKTHORNS.

Family RHAMNACEÆ.

BUCKTHORNS (Rhamnus).

Cascara (*Rhamnus purshiana*).

Varies from small tree to slender-stemmed shrub. Bark bitter, medicinal. Leaves blunt, oval, deeply ribbed with straight parallel veins. Usually an undergrowth on low river bottoms.

THE DOGWOODS.

Family CORNACEÆ.

DOGWOODS (Cornus).

WESTERN DOGWOOD (*Cornus nuttalli*).

Small tree, usually growing under other trees. Leaves broad, pointed, oval, ribbed with curved parallel veins. Large, showy white flowers. On low bottoms, the lower gentle mountain slopes, and along mountain streams.

THE HEATH FAMILY.

Family ERICACEÆ.

MADROÑAS (Arbutus).

MADROÑA (*Arbutus menziesii*).

Tree frequently low and shrubby, with conspicuous, smooth red-brown bark which often peels off in thin, irregular flakes, red branches, evergreen leaves, and bright coral-red berries. Along rivers. Occurrence rare in this region.

THE OLIVE FAMILY.

Family OLEACEÆ.

ASHES (Fraxinus).

OREGON ASH (*Fraxinus oregona*).

A tree usually of the swamps. Reaches 60 to 75 feet in height. Bark in fine ridges and furrows. Leaf compound, having five to seven leaflets. Seeds winged at one end. Western part of Cascades in valleys.

THE HONEYSUCKLE FAMILY.

Family CAPRIFOLIACEÆ.

ELDERBERRIES (Sambucus).

BLUE ELDERBERRY (*Sambucus glauca*).

Usually a many-stemmed shrub; rarely a tree 15 to 20 feet high. Compound leaves and pale bluish berries. Bottoms of canyons, valleys, slopes of mountain streams, and moist hillsides.

ADDITIONAL COPIES
OF THIS PUBLICATION MAY BE PROCURED FROM
THE SUPERINTENDENT OF DOCUMENTS
GOVERNMENT PRINTING OFFICE
WASHINGTON, D. C.
AT
10 CENTS PER COPY
∇

WASHINGTON : GOVERNMENT PRINTING OFFICE : 1920